*Their Father's Heirs*

THEIR FATHER'S HEIRS
Zelophehad's Daughters

Copyright © 2015 Cynthia Ekoh. All rights reserved. Except for brief quotations in critical publications or reviews, no part of this book may be reproduced in any manner without prior written permission from the publisher. Write: Permissions. Wipf and Stock Publishers, 199 W. 8th Ave., Suite 3, Eugene, OR 97401.

Resource Publications
An Imprint of Wipf and Stock Publishers
199 W. 8th Ave., Suite 3
Eugene, OR 97401

www.wipfandstock.com

ISBN 13: 978-1-62564-671-2

Manufactured in the U.S.A.                          04/06/2015

# Their Father's Heirs
## Zelophehad's Daughters

Cynthia Ekoh

RESOURCE *Publications* • Eugene, Oregon

# Acknowledgements

I THANK MY LORD JESUS for the inspiration to expound on this beautiful story that was recorded for our example. Many Christians that I have asked about Zelophehad were ignorant of his character. So it is with great pleasure that I present this obscure story from the Bible in vivid pictures in a way that you can relate to.

I appreciate my dear husband, Saint Ekoh, who is my teacher and pastor. Some of the elaboration in this book has come from his teachings in our church.

I appreciate everyone who read sample chapters of this book and gave me the push and encouragement to publish it. My godmother described this book as "loaded" because it is loaded with information from the Bible that you often do not give attention to. This is a most entertaining Bible story to be enjoyed by both young and old.

*Cynthia Ekoh*

# 1

TODAY WAS MILCAH'S EIGHTIETH day of life. Zelophehad, her father, stood with his wife, who was more relieved than excited, at the entrance of the tent of meeting. They were offering to YHWH a year-old lamb for a burnt offering to mark the end of her eighty-day isolation after the birth of their daughter. For her purification, she gave her preferred and difficult-to-get bird, a dove, as she always did. Zelophehad also gave an extra offering, surprising his wife. For months they had struggled to obtain a year-old male lamb without any blemish or defect for today. In addition, Zelophehad had complained so much about their dwindling livestock and so she was surprised to see the young bull handed over to her husband by his nephew. He had deliberately kept his wife in the dark about this second offering. Not because she had any problem with them giving all their livestock to YHWH, but to forestall her criticism of his motive. He had arranged with his nephew to quietly bring the young bull way behind them. From the corner of his left eye he could make out his wife's expression of surprise and concern. He suspected his wife knew exactly what the extra offering was for. The priest motioned for his extra offering with a knowing look at his daughter that said "I understand your plight." "Well for the love of God. This is my fourth daughter and not one son yet! It is certainly not a crime for me to be obviously desperate." Zelophehad brooded and let off a sigh working on his facial expression. He did not want the priest to know what just went through his mind or think that he came before YHWH with an attitude other than piety. He was going through this ritual for the fourth time, each time with growing desperation but he was still hopeful. Ironically, his brother Baruch would be presenting his fourth son in a couple of days on his fortieth day of life, half the length of time they had to observe for his daughter. It seemed every time he was having a baby, his brother Baruch was right behind him just like when they were children. Only this time he could not show off greater strength as the big brother. Surely this was the true test of a man's strength, thought Zelophehad, wishing it were possibly to switch babies like they used to exchange their wooden swords as boys.

Belonging to the fast-growing tribe of Manasseh, one of the wealthiest tribes, Zelophehad worried that he might not be able to keep his portion without a son. Since Egypt, every tribe had continued to grow and increase in number and in substance, but at this time the greatest gain was with the tribe of Manasseh. They had started out as the smallest in number but were growing so fast that the last census had them at over thirty thousand not counting their women and children. They were not the largest tribe but their growth was most significant, happening at a time when the tribes of Reuben, Simeon, Gad, and even Ephraim were losing large numbers of their men. Their increasing numbers was one thing that baffled and concerned him greatly. He knew that a lot of his people would castigate him or even curse him to sleep for calling what they think is a great blessing a concern. But when they left Egypt, they had been only six hundred thousand men in number and his tribe had been a little less than half the number they were now. His wonder was how they kept on increasing every day despite the harsh conditions and several wars in the wilderness. His concern was how such a large herd of people would be safely ushered into the promised land and when they get there, would the land be enough to go round. Moreover it was getting more and more difficult for them to move these days. They were able to actually sow and harvest because the time spent at their stops has increasingly lengthened.

The God of their fathers was definitely making good the blessings pronounced by Jacob on the twelve patriarchs many years ago. As a beneficiary of the noble patriarch Joseph, a sizeable portion of the nation's inheritance belonged to his tribe and he definitely did not want to lose out. He was a fourth-generation descendant and took great pride in his tribe. He was a firstborn just as his father, Hepher, was to his father, Gilead, the firstborn of Makir. As a matter of fact his name meant *firstborn*. The firstborn child was very important and the desire of every parent is that it be a male. Sons were a man's greatest assets in Israel. They were the ones to preserve their family name and inheritance for generations. They watched the gate. They went to wars. They died with pride in defense of their people and the land. The measure of your strength and capacity as a man was in the number of sons you have. Just the other day, Moses had commanded that all the firstborn males in the camp be counted. Zelophehad had been so mortified when one of the censoring Levites came by his tent asking if his newborn baby was a male. He did not need a reminder that yet again he had failed to bring forth an heir from his loins, someone to represent his house. With a very low voice he had respectfully told the Levite that his newborn baby was not a firstborn and left it at that.

His wife believed that he worried too much and almost daily reminded him that they had the most beautiful daughters in Israel. His wife was a wonderful, godly woman who sought nothing but his happiness. She has borne him four beautiful daughters but he needed to prove the authenticity of his manhood. Zelophehad had never failed any test of masculinity in his life. As a firstborn male in his family he had many privileges that his brothers did not. Growing up he had been the family's showcase. Oh how he loved those days as a boy, when he was always given the preference among his six brothers. Whether gifts, meals, opportunities, the first gets it first and most often gets the best. In Israel, every firstborn male whether of man or animal belonged to YHWH. And this identity automatically made them special, distinguishing them from their siblings. As a firstborn male, he had to be redeemed with a costly sacrifice. He smiled as he remembered taunting his brothers with that. Every time they contended with him in spiritual matters, he used to say to them, "I am redeemed, you are not, so let the redeemed of the Lord speak." To top it all, he gets a double portion of his family's inheritance. However, right now he did not feel that superiority. How he envied his brother Baruch who has had four sons in the same space of time he's had his four daughters. Seemingly it appears like a pitch of beauty against brawn with him and Baruch.

# Their Father's Heirs

Before their father Hepher died, he had called him and blessed him as the firstborn. One of the things he said to him was that his brothers were now his sons. His father's dying pronouncement had him wondering if it was just about him inheriting his father's role as the head of the family or was there more to it prophetically. His brothers were all grown men with families of their own. Even though he was the firstborn and head of their family, the truth was that the age gap between them was not significant. His mother had literally had babies every year. As boys and as young men, one could never tell who was the oldest or the youngest until they were told. His two sisters, the twins, who were between him and his second brother, Makir, were the ones that were mistaken for the babies of the family. Zelophehad was finding it harder as the days went by to exert himself as the head to his brothers. Not because he did not understand his role as the head of their family or did not want to live up to the role, but because he felt disqualified. Once upon a time he had been so confident and sure of himself. Where was that young man? The young man that knew he was a leader by divine design and never hesitated to be first whether in trouble or triumph. Maybe he had taken it for granted that just as he was first in everything it was also his birthright to be the first to show strength in procreation. Baruch, his youngest brother, had four sons, and each of his other brothers had more. He knew that it was only a matter of time before his brothers would begin to resent him. If he ended up without an heir, it meant that his portion of their family's wealth would be lost. No family or tribe likes depreciation of any form. Every family and tribe wants only increase. He did not want to be responsible for taking away from his family but rather wanted to live up to his name. He did not want to be a father to his brothers either, as his dead father had suggested. He desperately wanted to be a father, but a father only to the sons from his loins. He and his brothers grew up competing and contending with one another anyway, so he could not see them looking to him as their father now. He wanted only to lead as he had always done growing up and that was his focus right now. Zelophehad returned from his reverie as he heard the priest call out, "Son of Hepher , the Lord bless you and keep you; the Lord make his face shine upon you and be gracious to you; the Lord turn his face toward you and give you peace." He shook himself, mouthed, "Amen," and took his leave, wishing the priest had said "give you sons" rather than "peace."

## 2

Zelophehad was not only anxious about his lack of a son but worried about many things. They had embarked on this journey to the promised land some twenty years ago when Moses returned from his self-exile with a message of deliverance from YHWH. Moses was born an Israelite but grew up an Egyptian prince in the house of Pharaoh, where he was adopted. He got into trouble trying to identify with his true people, the Israelites. That cost him his royal privileges, resulting in his exile. Many of them had thought it an irony that the very palace that caused them so much pain would be the same one from which a savior would arise to deliver them. Well that was the very meaning of the name Moses if you were Hebrew. However, Pharaoh's daughter who adopted him had given him the name Moses, which to the Egyptians meant *son*. So depending on what side you were looking from, he was either Egypt's son or Israel's deliverer. He believed without a doubt that Moses was their "Deliverer."

Many of his people had found it difficult to believe this Israelite-Egyptian in the beginning, and he believed some still doubted today because of this never-ending journey to the promised land. He sometimes wondered what would have happened had members of Moses' family not been around to support his claims. Aaron his brother had been instrumental in convincing their people to follow Moses, and Miriam his sister had been the one who stood to prove his nativity to the doubting ones. Well they were the very ones that were closest to him and now assisted him with governing the people. Aaron his brother was the high priest, while Miriam was a highly respected prophetess and the only woman in leadership. She was a very influential woman, greatly admired by all the women, especially his wife, who wanted their daughters to be like Miriam. Though both Aaron and Miriam were older than Moses, who was their baby brother, yet they submitted to him as YHWH's chosen leader for Israel. Moreover, they belonged to the house of Levi, the respected priestly tribe, even though Moses grew up in the house of Pharaoh. For Zelophehad and many others it was the awesome acts and supernatural interventions which led to their deliverance that authenticated and proved Moses. He had vivid recollection of the time and all the events that had led to their escape from Egypt. He still had nightmares sometimes, of walking in the midst of that Red Sea. On dry land they had walked right in the midst of that sea, with walls of trembling water on either side looking tumultuous and ready to fall back into position. It had been as if the waters were literally held apart by a mighty invisible hand on either side as they walked through. It had been both a terrifying and exciting experience, like a dangerous adventure. He remembered some families who had been too terrified and would not follow the herd of people until much pleading and of course the approach of Pharaoh's soldiers had forced them into the waters. He remembered watching in amazement and horror as the same waters that had parted to give them passage had returned with such force. Pharaoh, his six hundred soldiers, chariots and horses had all disappeared before their very eyes. It was as if the whole of Egypt was wiped out. And it had happened so quickly, shortly after Moses had proclaimed to them, "The Egyptians you see today, you will see no more." It had been a miracle and the ultimate payback to Pharaoh who had believed he was a god unto himself and the people. The whole event from the first plague to the last they saw of the Egyptians had been a humiliation of all their gods. It was established that their hundreds of gods were no match for the One God of Israel. They had not only escaped from their slave masters but they had left Egypt a very wealthy people. There was no family in Israel without valuables. Gold, silver, bronze, every kind of gemstones and any valuable asset that could be named, they had it. They had more than enough to buy land and anything else that they would need to settle in Canaan. Perhaps this was why he worried so much, Zelophehad thought. "Without an heir, what is the benefit of all my possessions?" It was not enough to have possessions. It was commonly believed and recited among them that the righteous leave inheritance for their children's children, but the wicked are cut off, never to be heard of. He had reassured himself time and time again that he was no wicked man and believed he would be counted among the righteous. "Without an heir you are no better than a pauper," his mother's favorite line seemed to invade his thoughts. But not for long, as his wife's sweet voice interrupted. "My Lord, I see that you have deceived me." They were walking back home with their baby, Hoglah, wrapped up so completely in swaddling clothes that he could not even see her face. He cleared his throat, buying time as he thought carefully of what to say to his wife. He did not want her to think that the reassurance he spent time giving her that morning meant nothing. He meant everything he had said to her earlier in the day when she woke up crying and worried. "I just wanted to give an extra offering to the Lord. Who knows, he just might smile down on me with a son sooner that you think." She glanced at his face, searching his soul through his eyes as only she knew how. He was always cautious with his wife because she understood his expressions and actions more than she did his Hebrew. "I will tell you. You are desperate for a son but you are an honorable man. You intend to keep your promise to me and our daughters and I love you but . . ." She paused looking very serious. He turned to face her stopping in his track. They had taken the less busy path home, the tracks behind the tents, so he could afford the luxury of some privacy with his wife. He put his two hands on her shoulders to stop her in her track and looked into her face. She looked down smiling, too shy to look into his face directly. He had known his wife for fifteen years and yet there were still moments like this one. She looked down at his feet and continued, ". . . You can always change your mind you know and I will still love you." "Woman, are you speaking the truth! Would you still love me when the other woman mocks and insults you for something you have no control over? Would you still love me when she makes your life miserable because I love you more than her? Would you still love me when peace no longer reigns in our home because of some strange woman? Would you . . ." They jumped as they heard footsteps creep upon them. It was a young man and a maiden holding hands. The young man waived and shouted a greeting respectfully while the young maiden snatched her hand away from his hand, obviously hiding her face behind her veils. Zelophehad took a cue from the approaching couple, grabbed his wife's hand, and they continued their journey home. "Let's give the young people some privacy and I hope they are pledged to be married. We have had our days."

It was not unusual to find young lovers along the paths behind the tents. This was one of the largest camps they have ever set, yet they seemed to have not enough space. You were always sure to bump into people anywhere and everywhere around the tents even on the Sabbath. If you wanted privacy, you remained in your tents or went to the mountains, hills, or bushes surrounding the camp. The only people with complete privacy, which of course was not by choice, were the offenders and the lepers. As much as he coveted some more privacy, he cringed at the thought of such complete isolation from the camp. Such had been the fate of the greatest woman in the camp—Miriam. Some years ago she had been isolated for leprosy, a curse that had come upon her for daring to challenge her brother Moses. They were a people governed by laws given to Moses directly by YHWH. They were different from the surrounding nations who envied their organization and culture. They had courts and judges to settle their disputes. They had a good system of justice that worked well for the people. Moses elected elders from all the tribes who were assigned to oversee the people in divisions of tens, fifties, hundreds, and thousands just like their army was structured. The overall judge, however, remained Moses, to whom difficult cases were presented. For the Moabites, the Amorites, the Amalekites, and the Cushites—the nations surrounding them—it was different. It was survival of not only the fittest but the roughest. Barbaric and unclean, they called them and were forbidden by the law to marry from these nations. Over the years they had had families come from these nations to beg for citizenship in Israel. Some qualified and many were rejected based on a number of conditions required by their laws. It was good to live in a community with laws. Egypt had been lawless. The Pharaohs were the law. They maimed, killed, and did about anything at their whims and wills. Israel had laws and regulations regarding every aspect of living. Food, drink, housing, marriage, birth, genders, death, diseases, crimes, slavery, farming, inheritance, and the list goes on. They had restitution and death penalty depending on the offense. Eye for an eye, tooth for a tooth. Life for a life. Even their animals were not exempted. He had once watched his brother Makir's leg deliberately broken as payment for his neighbor's fractured limb, which he had been responsible for in the course of a fight. His friend Ramah, a Cushite turned Israelite, often argued that their people were no better than the other nations but were forced by the laws to behave. Zelophehad's comeback was always that it did not matter which came first, whether the law or the good behavior. It was peace that mattered. At least he was sure that a man could not kill him and go free. He was sure that no man would encroach on his territory and get away with it. He was sure no priestess would demand for one of his daughters to be burnt in a fire as a sacrifice to a worthless idol. He was sure no man could forcefully take his wife from him. He was a man who loved predictability. At least they were not likely to wake up one day and be told that they were no longer bona fide members of their community. They were a nation now. They were God's special people, they were Israel! The mention of their name terrified many nations. Clearly they had heard of the dread they left in Egypt and their dealings with the Amalekites. Only their destination Canaan troubled him. They were informed that giants filled the land and great walls surrounded their cities. For twenty-five years now they have been waiting on this promised land. The land they were to claim was extensive. It included the land of the Amorites, Hitittites, Hivittites, Perizzites, Jebusites, and of course the focus—Canaan. Maybe if they had at least conquered the extensions by now he would worry less. But here they were, it seemed, stranded in Paran for now. Maybe the several wars they had faced so far was part of YHWH's plan to prepare them for the giants of Canaan, only Moses could tell him he believed. His thought focused on Moses at the moment as he tried to understand the person he was made of. He was in awe of this man. There was just something about Moses. He thought of his calm, his carriage, his courage, his humility, his conducts, his intimacy with YHWH, even his looks. He looked the same as he had over twenty years ago when he began to lead them. His brother, Aaron, the high priest, was not so lucky. The four years between them seemed more like forty years. Yet all the weight and burden of their nation was on this man. To be fair to Aaron, he had undergone a lot, losing two sons at the same time and having to live a very restricted life as a high priest.

## 3

Zelophehad smiled as he approached the entrance of his tent and heard his daughters' loud chatter and his mother's nagging voice asking them to be quiet so she could hear the footsteps approaching their tent. He did not know how she did it, but his mother could tell with almost perfect precision the person approaching their tent by their footsteps. She knew when it was his or his siblings. She could tell if it was bad or good tidings that was coming with a footstep. He often took advantage of her forecast. He was always prepared for every visitor. His mother came out of the tent with his daughters and the first thing she said to him was, "Any word from the priest?" A feeling of annoyance began to well up inside him as he understood exactly what she was talking about. She had asked him this same question three years ago when he had returned with his wife and Hoglah, his third daughter. She could at least have started with welcoming them or asking how it went. But that was his mother, never one to waste time on pleasantries. She seemed to have gotten worse with age. His wife kissed his mother and quickly vanished into their tent, ushering the girls in with her as she mumbled something about feeding the baby. He knew how much his wife hated such confrontation, especially in the presence of their daughters. He schooled his expressions and scooped up his third daughter, Hoglah, laughing as she shouted in glee. He was always careful not to get into any heated argument with his mother in the presence of his children. He did not want them growing to think that they can talk back to their mother and him. He waited for them to enter the tent and then he turned to his mother with his worst scowl. When his mother saw the look in his eyes she reached out to touch him affectionately saying, "Well you know how much I am so concerned about you. You are my first son and I do not want you cheated. I had sons and all your brothers have sons so we know the source of this problem. All I am saying is that you should take another wife since she cannot give you a son." This only made Zelophehad angrier and he wished for the umpteenth time that his mother would just go live with any of his siblings and get off his case. He had had just about enough. He replied to her slowly, "Imah, I have told you over and over that I would do anything to have a son but that. I love my wife and the girls. While I wait for a son, I will train my daughters to be strong, confident women who will make history in Israel." His mother snorted. "How will they do that may I ask? Can they go to war and defend our nation? Can they give you sons that will carry on your name? You know they will be married off to some men and leave your house desolate." "Imah!!!!" Zelophehad growled and walked away from his mother and his tent as she continued her tirade, shouting after him, "Don't wait for a son, get a son you hear me." Walking away briskly, he decided to go far away from the quadrangle of tents into the nearby wilderness to cool off. He tried hard all the time not to dishonor his mother even though she made him angry enough to do just that. He was determined to live a very long life. He would not allow his mother to cut it short for him by causing him to dishonor her. "What a day!" Zelophehad hissed under his breath. He had woken up to his wife's tears early in the morning and had spent an hour convincing her that all was well with their family. She had feared that he was going to give in this time to his mother's counsel and take another woman after their fourth girl. For the love of God, they were still in the middle of nowhere. No sight of the promised land. They were nomads moving from one valley and mountain to another at the dictates of Moses. His tent was already crowded with a wife, four daughters, and his mother. Why would he bring in another woman who may very well continue the tradition? He believed sons were gifts from YHWH and it had nothing to do with the woman. He had spent time this morning reassuring his wife, and now this conversation with his mother may very well have incited another bout of anxieties in his poor wife. His wife was not just his wife but was also kin. She was his second cousin. And even if she were no kin, he knew he would still love her and honor her as much. He did not even know her growing up until they were pledged to be married. It was his father who chose her after a careful search for the most suitable wife for his firstborn. His mother, sisters, and brothers had approved of her from the first day she was introduced to them as his wife. She had a wonderful relationship with his sisters and even his mother. Though he knew without a doubt that no woman could take her place with his family, nevertheless he was maintaining his stand to honor her. After all, Abraham refused to take another wife besides Sarah even without any child. And Abraham was their father. All he wanted was for his mother to understand and respect his decision. "I will continue to do what I know to do and wait for YHWH to smile down upon me with a son. And I hope very soon," he said out loud, talking to himself. His situation appeared peculiar to him as he truly could not name another man in his tribe or other tribes facing this same dilemma. There must be at least one, he pondered. Many men in his age group had more than one wife, he realized, solely for this same reason—sons. Some in this bid had defiled many girls, something he refused to do. He was too honorable for that. "Jehovah will satisfy the desire of my heart. I am blessed to belong to the tribe of Manasseh. I am not the least of my brethren. My quivers are filled with sons. I will make it to the promised land and my inheritance will not be taken from me. . ." As he recited his favorite prayer lines, Zelophehad felt some calmness return to him. He decided to go by his olive groves and to see how Kish was doing and to get his mind off his unsettling thoughts.

On getting to his farm, he found Kish with his torso bare, sweating profusely as he worked. He watched him a while and as always felt compassion for the boy. He had bought him three years ago from his uncle, a very harsh man. His plan was to liberate him after six years as permitted by the law. That was the only way he could help the boy. Kish's father, a Cushite slave, was bought many years ago by Zelophehad's uncle who also gave him a crippled Hebrew girl for wife. Kish and his sister, the result of this union, had automatically belonged to their father's master. Kish's father had gotten his freedom after many years but was not allowed to leave with his family under the law. Kish had been devastated and adversely affected by his father abandoning them. He had become defiant, which had led to a lot of suffering at the hands of his master. He was always being flogged for one reason or another. On one occasion he was caught trying to run away and was given the beating of his life. It was at this point that Zelophehad came into the picture, bargaining with his uncle with much pleading for the boy. He had paid twice the price he was worth. His brothers and mother had teased him mercilessly. They credited his benevolence to his lack of a son. Maybe they were right, because every time he looked at the boy, fatherly emotions welled up. Maybe God will honor his good deed, a slave boy for a son. "Did you get off as much of the mildew as possible?" Kish straightened up and bowed in greeting. His face tanned by daily exposure to the sun made him look more like a Cushite than a Hebrew. "Take a break and go get something to drink and eat before you faint." He did not stop what he was doing immediately as you would expect of a child his age but took his time to finish brushing off the mildew from the shrub he was dealing with. Neither did he show any excitement, which worried Zelophehad a great deal. He made sure he did not give Kish more work than was appropriate for a boy his age. He talked to him gently. He allowed him enough freedom to go and come as he liked, as he had allowed him to continue to live in his family tent with his mother and sister. Kish was not used to acts of kindness and no matter how Zelophehad tried to change his perception, the boy still did not trust people, especially men. "Go on. I said take a break. Go on home and get something to drink and eat. I will continue where you left off." Kish was only fourteen but looked and behaved like a man. He was sturdy and muscular, scarred in the face and on his back. His forlorn looks of a beaten cub had Zelophehad's heart melt every time he looked at him. In those black pebbled eyes was pain and sadness that should never have been his. He was too young. At his age Zelophehad remembered being carefree and happy. He strongly wanted to help him heal and learn to trust again. He had three more years to go and he would become a free Hebrew. His mother was one and he was being raised as a Hebrew. Zelophehad planned not only to give him his freedom but a life afterward if Kish would allow him. His mother and sister still officially belonged to Zelophehad's uncle but he would help him redeem them. He hoped the boy will not take off in search of his father like he attempted before. If he did, there was nothing he could do to stop him as he would be a free man by then. He knew how he had been with his own father and could not imagine growing up without one.

They were battling with early signs of mildew attack and were trying to get rid of as many oil spots as possible from the foliage before they became powdery and messed up the berries. Zelophehad made a lot of money from olive oil, an essential commodity that was needed by all. Their lamps were fueled by olive oil. The tabernacle consumed half of their production because the lamps in the tabernacle must be kept lighted at all times. He was also planning to harvest some olive wood, which is valued for ornamental work, before they relocated. Because of their increasing stay at their camps nowadays, many of them were able to cultivate the land around them. Vineyards and olive groves were common, even though sometimes they would have to abandon farmlands before they could harvest their crops. Some people had simply refused to venture into farming because of this. For him, he would continue to plant just as they continued to marry and have children. His only setback was lack of enough hands. His wife who was his main help had been in confinement for eighty days, but thank God it was over now. He would begin to enjoy her company again on the farm.

# 4

BACK IN THEIR TENT Zelophehad's wife was feeding her baby Milcah and singing as she did so. Her three daughters surrounded her to listen and learn as she sang the song of deliverance. *"I will sing unto the Lord for he has triumphed gloriously, the horse and the rider thrown into the sea . . ."* Noah, clinging to her mother's side, asked her to tell them again the story behind the song. The song was popularly known among the Israelites as the song of Moses and Miriam. It was first sung at the crossing of the Red Sea, spontaneously composed by Miriam and Moses as they led the people to give thanks to YHWH for their deliverance. Even though she had no clear recollection of what had happened at the Red Sea because she had been about Noah's age then, Zelophehad's wife like many Israelite knew every detail of the great testimony of their deliverance from Egypt. She began her story with the time when Moses fearlessly went to Pharaoh, king of Egypt, to demand the release of all the Israelites. She recounted how the king of Egypt had proved stubborn, playing tricks on Moses. She recounted all the different plagues YHWH rained down on the Egyptians as punishment for Pharaoh's stubbornness. She explained carefully the last plague that broke Pharaoh, not wanting to terrify her daughters. The girls all laughed and clapped their hands in delight as their mother ended the story and their baby sister belched at the same time. "But Imah, how did our fathers get to Egypt and why did they have to go to such a mean place in the first place?" Noah asked. "Abbah told me that it was because YHWH planned it to be so," Mahlah, the firstborn, quickly responded before their mother could gather her thoughts. Wiser than her sisters by virtue of her age, plus having heard the story more times than they had, Mahlah looked to their mother for confirmation. Her mother looked at her with pride and smiled and started another chapter of the story.

Zelophehad's wife, who was a pious woman, loved telling these stories not only to entertain her daughters but to remind herself time and time again of the greatness of the God they served. It gave her strength and hope for the future. "Well girls, you know that Abraham our father had Isaac, and Isaac had Jacob, who became the father of the twelve patriarchs. Now because the patriarchs were jealous of their little brother Joseph being their father's favorite, they sold him as a slave into Egypt." Noah, who was always trailing her sister in a bid to outdo, again interrupted her, exclaiming, "Now I know why our fathers became slaves in Egypt. It was because Joseph, the first Israelite to get to Egypt, went there as a slave!" Their mother smiled and continued her story, marveling at this interesting show of intelligent reasoning by her eight-year-old daughter. "Well, my lamb, I am not sure about that, but God was with him and rescued him from all the troubles and challenges he faced in Egypt. Joseph found favor with people everywhere he went, even with Pharaoh the king of Egypt. The king made him a ruler in Egypt, his second in command. Somewhere along the line, a great famine struck all Egypt and Canaan, bringing great suffering, and our people could not find food." Mahlah looking confused asked, "You said Egypt and Canaan, where did Jacob and his sons live?" "Oh they used to live in the land of Canaan, but as foreigners before they migrated to Egypt. Anyway, under the rule of Joseph, Egypt was able to conserve a large reserve of food, and all the surrounding nations went to Egypt for food. When Jacob, Joseph's father, heard that there was food in Egypt, he sent his sons down to Egypt to buy food. So the patriarchs visited Egypt, bought the food they needed without realizing that the man in charge was their own very brother Joseph. On their second visit, Joseph revealed himself to his brothers, and Pharaoh learned about Joseph's family. After this, Joseph sent for his father and his whole family, seventy-five in all. And so Jacob and the twelve patriarchs lived and died in Egypt, though they were not buried there but at Shechem. Our people continued to live in Egypt and increased greatly in number and were very prosperous until another king who knew nothing about Joseph became the ruler of Egypt. The new Pharaoh was a wicked man, oppressing our people and making them his slaves. He was so evil that he ordered for every newborn male baby belonging to the Israelites to be killed." At this the girls gasped. Hoglah, the youngest of the three, began to cry, while Mahlah burst out vehemently, "That is so evil! Imagine if we had to lose our baby Milcah." Their mother held on tightly to her baby and shuddered. "Well we know that YHWH is faithful in making ways of escape for his people at all times. The story gets better. It was at this time that Moses was born and his mother was able to hide him for three months in his father's house until she devised a plan to keep her baby safe. She put Moses in a basket into the river Nile where Pharaoh's daughter was having a bath. The princess heard the baby cry and sent her servants to pick him up. She adopted him as her son and she raised him as her own. Moses was brought up and educated as an Egyptian prince. He learned the art of medicine, literature, art, and architecture. He lived a privileged life while all our people suffered greatly at the hands of the Egyptians." Mahlah, with a dreamy look on her little face, interrupted her mother wanting to know if Moses' wife was an Egyptian. She believed that Zipporah was the most beautiful woman that she had ever seen in her young life. "Well Mother, is she an Egyptian?" "No, my sweet lamb. Zipporah is from Midian, though they are all called Cushites. The Egyptians, Ethiopians, and Midianites originated from Cush. And you, my dove, are more beautiful. Now one day when Moses was all grown, he decided to visit Goshen, in Lower Egypt, where the Israelites resided. On his first visit to his people, he met an ugly scene. He saw an Egyptian man beating a helpless Israelite to the point of death. Moses was so enraged at the injustice that he killed the Egyptian and buried him secretly. Of course the news went round and a lot of our people were happy and proud of him for standing up for his true kinsmen, but some of them however did not appreciate Moses. Not too long afterward on another day, Moses came upon two Israelites fighting and tried to reconcile them. But to his surprise, the man who had initiated the fight was horrible to Moses. He pushed him aside, asking who had made him their ruler and judge. He accused Moses of wanting to kill him like he did the Egyptian. When Moses heard that, he was so disappointed and of course was afraid. He feared that the news would get to Pharaoh if people continued to talk about it so publicly, so he fled from Egypt. He had thought the people would accept and appreciate him for being on their side but they did not. So he fled to Midian where he met his wife Zipporah. He settled there as a shepherd working with his father-in-law Jethro and he started his family. Moses was in Midian for forty years, a completely different man from the young Egyptian prince that fled from Egypt. Well one day while he was minding his routine business as a shepherd, YHWH stopped him in his tracks. YHWH sent him back to Egypt to rescue us." "Imah, is it true that Moses sees YHWH all the time?" Noah the inquisitive one asked. "Oh yes, my lamb. How do you think we made it so far? Moses is a holy man and a great prophet, without him there will be no Israel. . ." Her voice faded as she became emotional at this point. So many things she could not explain to her daughters because of their age. Even for an adult, it was difficult to understand it all. YHWH has revealed himself to them in many ways, yet they really did not know him like Moses did. At Mount Sinai they had come that close to seeing him when he requested to meet with them for the first time. Moses had prepared them and took them to the foot of the mountain. It had been the most terrifying experience. The mountain had trembled so violently when a great fire suddenly descended on it. Moses had announced that as the presence of the Lord, but all they had seen was smoke erupting from a furnace from the top of the mountain. And they had heard a thundering when he spoke to Moses, who had been the only person who had gone closer. He had disappeared into the smoke on top of the mountain. On another occasion, when Moses went to receive the tablets of law, Aaron and his sons with the seventy elders were given another chance to see him. This time they saw only a part of him, underneath his feet. What they have described as a pavement of sapphire stone covered with the most brilliant blue sky. There had been so much brilliant light from it that they could not gaze directly. Only Moses again had seen him close up. No one, including Moses, had been able to describe what he looks like exactly. But one thing had been made clear to them when Moses returned from that meeting, with his face radiating blinding light so that he had to wear a veil for days: no one can behold him because he is covered in blinding light.

Zelophehad's wife returned from her reverie to conclude her story but was interrupted this time by the sound of a footstep approaching their tent. "I can hear your father approaching. It is time for you girls to settle down and prepare for the evening." She waived them to their corner of the room. She went behind a curtain to put Milcah, who was fast asleep, in her crib at their corner of the room, which was a good distance from the girls. She looked in the far corner south of their sizeable tent and was pleased to see that her mother-in-law looked settled in for the night. She needed all the privacy tonight to talk with her husband, especially after what had transpired between him and his mother earlier. As she thought of what her mother-in-law must have said to him, she began to wonder if she was not being selfish. Yes, she would rather remain her husband's only wife, but how about him. How long could he stand the pressure and his mother's taunting. It was a different thing when the taunting came from outsiders, but when it comes from an insider, how does one escape. Since she had Milcah, there had not been a day gone by that her mother-in-law had not make a reference to their lack of a male child in the house. She could never bring herself to despise her mother-in-law no matter how her acrid comments hurt. She was more concerned about her husband's state of mind. If he is unhappy, she is miserable. It had always been like that for her since the day she married him.

# 5

Zelophehad entered his tent still very heavy, weighed down by his own thoughts. After he'd left his farmland he had visited with his brother Baruch not wanting to face his mother too soon. They had taken a walk around the camp and talked. As they walked past the tent of meeting, they had noticed a bevy of activity around the tent. The Levites were standing at different posts, guarding the sacred tent to prevent anybody from coming too close. Inside the courtyard were the council of elders and the priests in a meeting with Moses. There was a palpable air of anxiety all around the camp. As they walked the camp they saw anxious faces, men in groups discussing the same thing—the ongoing meeting. The whole camp was a quadrangle set up in division of threes while the tent of meeting was erected in the center. To the west of the tabernacle were the tribes of Ephraim, Benjamin, and Manasseh. To the east were the tribes of Judah, Issachar, and Zebulun. To the south were the Reubenites, Simeonites, and the Gaddites. To the north were the camps for the tribes of Dan, Naphtali, and Asher. The tent of meeting was erected in the heart of the camp with carefully measured distances between it and the tents around it. The tent of meeting was a place prohibited to everyone except the spiritual leaders. The Levites were camped around the tabernacle as a protective edge to keep the people away. To the east of the tabernacle, toward the sunrise, were the tents belonging to Moses and those of Aaron and his sons right in front of the tent of meeting. With their increasing numbers they found themselves requiring more and more land space as they travelled from place to place in the wilderness. Since they had embarked on their journey after crossing the Red Sea, they had had the presence of YHWH lead them in the form of a cloud of smoke in the day and in the form of a cloud of fire at night. Whenever and wherever the cloud overhead them stopped, they camped there, and whenever it lifted they moved on. The cloud was currently settled at Paran, south of Canaan, and Zelophehad, like many others, was dying to move again. There had been too many delays. The old amongst them were tired of moving while the young were only too eager to move just as they arrived at a place. Before they embarked on this journey, Moses and men knowledgeable about the geography of the region had studied and predicted that this journey should take them no longer than two months. Since then he had married and produced four children. His wife had been no older than their first daughter, Mahlah, when they had began this journey. It was about the twenty-fifth year now and there was no Canaan in sight. If only they could turn back the hands of time. Disobedience and rebellion has cost them almost three decades on a journey that should have taken them three months. From the talks in the air, the ongoing solemn meeting was about another possible mission to Canaan. Over twenty years ago, shortly after they had entered the Desert of Sinai, Moses had instructed the heads of the tribes to elect one man each from their tribes for a mission to the promised land. The twelve men had been sent as spies into Canaan. Zelophehad had thought it too dangerous and not a wise move then. "Why risk lives and the possibility of being discovered by the Canaanites?" But now he had a different mindset. He was desperate for this journey to end. Should he be picked this time around if that were possible, he would gladly go. At least he would see the land for himself, he thought. He thought of his late cousin Gaddi who was one of the spies that had been sent to Canaan. He had not particularly cared for Gaddi when he lived. But now he felt sorry for the miserable way he had died along with all the other nine men. The twelve spies had returned from Canaan after forty days bearing two contradicting reports. Joshua and Caleb, the only two of the twelve spies still alive today, had brought a good report. They had reported that Canaan was just as YHWH had said—filled with good things. They were the only two among the twelve spies who had believed that they could take the land. The other ten men, including his cousin Gaddi, had given a contrary view that caused many of them to fear. "A land filled with giants!" they had reported, and that had been the genesis of their troubles. The news had resulted in fear, dissension, and rebellion. The ten spies with all their supporters had been struck down before their eyes by a terrible plague from YHWH. He winced as memories of those dreadful events flooded his mind, making everything look bleak. He hoped that Moses would have some good news for them after this meeting. They were bound to hear from Gamaliel, the head of their tribe, very soon. If it is another mission to Canaan, he was sure he could never convince Gamaliel and his tribesmen to make him their representative. They all appeared to overlook him these days, the reason was not lost on him. It was the same reason why he was not actively involved in their warfare. He was a strong and skilled soldier, better than his six brothers who were high ranking officials in the army. He had been celebrated for his exploits during the war with the Amalekites years ago. That was a war to remember. They had been led by Joshua who was the captain then over the whole army of Israel. They had fought their hearts out and returned drunk with victory only to learn that it was Moses who fought and won the actual battle. YHWH had instructed Moses to raise his rod while they fought, and as long as his rod was raised they had the upper hand. When his arm went down they were overcome by the Amalekites. And so Moses had to raise his rod up for almost three days while they fought. He could not eat, drink, or move. At a point, they had to support his arms with stones and help him stand as he grew tired and weak. It was like a beautiful flower whose beauty is seen and appreciated by all, but the root which draws water and nutrients from the soil for that beauty is not seen. They had countless such exciting spiritual operations recorded. Coming out of the past into the present, he looked out for his wife as he entered into his tent knowing very well that she would be anxiously waiting for him after all that had happened earlier with his mother.

He entered his tent and his wife came straight into his arms in a comforting embrace. She touched his forehead as if to erase the frown he was wearing. "My lord you are at it again, worrying yourself to death. Come and sit. Your food has been on the fire waiting for you. Eat, ease your mind and share with me all that plagues you. I have stories of our daughters to share with you too. You would not believe how intelligent these girls are at their young age." He knew his wife was trying as always to get his mind off his worries. He was always telling her that worrying was part of life. It was a man's lot to worry as long as he continued to live in the land of the living. He recounted to his wife the speculations about another mission to Canaan. He told her about Kish. He told her about the mildew attack on their vine. She offered him words of encouragement as he talked until he told her how much he would love to represent his tribe on the mission but feared he was overlooked because of you know what. She argued that his feelings about being left out for lack of sons were not justified. Even though this was one of the qualities that made his wife appealing, for the moment he resented her "holier than thou" attitude. You could never get her to criticize anybody or anything that had to do with their leadership. It was one of the reasons he felt his mother was able to get away with things with his wife. She was too respectful, too humble, and would rather suffer in silence than speak out. And this was not because she did not know her rights. She was one who would rather give up her rights for peace. It amused him that she, however, had chosen to admire the influential and outspoken Miriam. Rumors abounded that Miriam had a great degree of control over the men in her life, a little too much for a woman. Even though she was seven years older than Moses and four years older than Aaron, she was still a woman. Everyone considered her a woman that knew how to make things happen in their nation. Miriam's son Hur had recently been ordained to work closely with Moses and Aaron even though his father was not of the tribe of Levi. Could Hur be under training to perhaps take over Moses leadership some day? He wondered but refrained from sharing this thought with his wife. Between Miriam and his wife, he would choose Miriam anytime for his daughters. He prayed that they would grow up to be more like Miriam rather than their mother even though he loved his wife's sweet and gentle spirit. He decided to end the political discussion with his wife, planning to visit his friends Helon or Enan the next day. Helon was one of the non-Israelites who had followed them out of Egypt where he had also been a slave. Enan was an Egyptian who had joined them by virtue of marriage to a Hebrew woman. The non-Israelites among them were condescendingly referred to as "rabble" and were known to initiate and cause most of the troubles in the camp. They were always the first to grumble, standing up to the leaders on many occasions. There was the time when they had instigated a near riot in the camp because of meat. They had complained about the miraculous manna they receive every morning and demanded meat. The manna was their lifesaving bread that started to drop from the sky at a time when they would have died of hunger in the desert of sin. He marveled at their act of ingratitude and repented for the thousandth time. What came over us then? He still could not understand how the same people who nearly died from lack of food would dare complain and reject the only available food. Oh how they had infuriated Moses. Yet at the end of the day, the same Moses had interceded for them and YHWH had given them quails for meat for forty days. For over twenty years now the manna had continued to fall like dew every morning except on Sabbaths. On the eve of every Sabbath, each family was allowed to gather twice the stipulated portion. It was a miracle no one could explain. Every morning, you gathered no more nor less than the stipulated quantity of manna no matter how much you hoarded. It remained one omer per person. By noon, when the sun waxed strong, the excess or uneaten manna simply melted away. When they left Egypt over twenty years ago, they had brought with them their herds and flocks of livestock, but then as they continued to journey in the arid desert of Sinai for so long, their livestock quickly dwindled away. It was a different story now, as they had been able to replenish their livestock from spoils of wars over the years. They now reared some of the finest cattle and sheep thanks to their nomadic lifestyle. As if she was in his thoughts, she stated rather than asked, "You got that young bull from Helon, didn't you. I wish we knew how he was always constantly able to make his animals reproduce so quickly."

He knew his wife, just like his mother, did not like his close association with the likes of Helon and Enan, but they were good friends. They were the only ones he could discuss plainly with, without feeling condemned. His mother was always lamenting this and making nasty comments. She had told him more than he cared to count that one day he would get into trouble by virtue of his relationship with his rabble friends. His mother had little tolerance for the foreigners in their midst no matter that they were no longer regarded as foreign but as part of them. She called them "the grumblers," refusing to accept them as Israelites. Zelophehad, turning his attention again to his wife, asked about what she wanted to tell him about his daughters. He knew he had mixed feelings a lot of times about his daughters, but he could not deny his love for them. He loved them and had hopes and dreams that they would grow up to be relevant in their time. Hearing about his daughters reminded him of his promise to begin to give them some lessons in self-defense. If they had been boys, this would have been the time to begin their military training. All the males in the camp from the age of twenty were trained soldiers, ready for war at any time, with the exception of the Levites and the aged. He listened with a smile as his wife told him about Mahlah's analytical mind and reminded him that in a couple of years she would become Bat Mitzvah. He liked the part about her brilliant mind, commenting on that but ignored the part about Bat Mitzvah. He was proud to hear how intelligent and articulate his nine-year-old Noah was. He frowned when told that Hoglah, who was seven, was overly emotional. He wondered how the baby Milcah will turn out. He wished strongly in his heart though that the next one they would have would be a boy. "Lord, just one fine, strong boy!" he mouthed without a sound, looking up with a plea. "Amen," responded his wife who knew he had just made a request when he rolled his eyes upward. She assumed his request was for their daughters. She herself made requests all the time for her daughters. She prayed that they would grow up unmatched in beauty and be godly women. She prayed that they would find men like their father as husbands to love and cherish them.

# 6

MILCAH WAS ONE YEAR and six months and his wife was pregnant again. Zelophehad was very happy and felt blessed that YHWH had put another baby in his wife's womb earlier than he had expected. He strongly believed it was the son he'd prayed for. He was tempted to secretly employ the service of a diviner from the neighboring town of the Jebusites, but his wife would not hear of it. And after he did some soul searching he had repented of that and gave a guilt offering. His wife had lectured him to the point of disgrace. He was supposed to be the spiritual leader for his family and here he was defecting. It must be his association with Helon and Enan, he decided, not willing to take full blame. He had resorted to spending serious time with his wife doing nothing but speaking to the baby in her womb. He not only declared every day that this baby would be a son but prayed that he would be a great soldier. He prayed that he would be a celebrated captain like Joshua, who is greatly admired by every person in the camp. His wife jokingly told him that he was fast becoming a prophet. Well he felt he needed all the prophetic anointing now. Often when prophets prophesied the birth of particular children, they ended up great. Miriam was known to have prophesied the birth of her brother Moses when her parents did not even plan to have any more children because of Pharaoh's death decree. It appeared that the call was already upon Miriam at that tender age of seven. Moses was born and he was the greatest man in their midst. "Well another great man is on the way and that is my son," Zelophehad thought out loud to his wife, who had her head in his lap. He'd told his wife that he would prove his mother wrong this time. He even planned to name his son Hepher, after his father, to make his mother jealous. He would probably have named one of the girls after her if she had been more supportive, he rationalized. As he continued to prophesy, he stretched his hand over his wife's belly, but she jumped up suddenly, crying, "My lord, I feel a sharp pain in my belly, please take your hand off." He looked up into her face and saw that she was wincing. His heart skipped a beat and he began to fear the worst. "Let me lie back for some time, please get your mother." "Should I get the midwives instead?" "No, not now," she answered, wincing again in pain. Zelophehad left immediately to look for his mother, who had gone visiting his sister not too far from them. He got hold of Mahlah first to stay with her mother. He wished Mahlah was through her training in midwifery. He and his wife had decided for her to begin midwifery training even before she became a Bat Mitzvah. It was a common practice with them. They had young girls who assisted and understudied the older midwives. Some of them could do most of the things their teachers could do even before they were fully qualified. It was thirteen-year-old Sarai, their neighbor, who had helped his brother's wife six months ago all by herself. By the time Zelophehad was returning with his mother to his tent, Noah was running toward him. Out of breath she announced, "Mother is bleeding!" He ran in panic into the tent. He saw that Mahlah had her lying on her side and was rubbing her mother's lower back as she screamed in pain. Zelophehad was so afraid he went right back out to get an experienced midwife. He moved like a man whose house was on fire and for him it felt like that. He feared that his wife could lose this pregnancy and he was convinced it must be a boy, otherwise why was this happening to them. His wife had had four pregnancies and there was never any bleeding before term. He had heard and seen women lose pregnancies like this. But his wife had no such history, so why now and why with his son. Was it his fault? Was the attention he gave bringing harm? "The Lord has said we will not cast our young. I will not lose my son," he began to recite frantically as he approached the tent of the nearest midwife. She was Mahlah's teacher, and one of the best in the camp. He met one of the midwife's daughters, and before she could greet him, he made known his mission. The young lady ran inside their tent to get her mother while he waited with clenched, whitened fist. He became cross and impatient as he waited for what seemed like an eternity for the midwife to come out of her tent. The moment she showed up, he began walking very quickly back to his tent, glancing over his shoulder with every stride to make sure she was coming behind him. This was the son he had been waiting for, he was sure of it. Right now he would give even his life to save his unborn son. His wife still had about three moons to go before delivery.

They arrived at his tent and he ushered the midwife in to join his mother and Mahlah, but he stayed outside, pacing the front of his tent. He could hear the midwife giving instructions as she took over. No sooner, Mahlah was out running toward the midwife's tent to pick up some herb she was requesting. He watched his daughter run and was proud of her sense of urgency with the situation, unlike her teacher who had wasted his time. She was back with a bag in her hand before he could take his tenth breath. She paused in her track in front of the tent when she saw him, but he quickly motioned for her to proceed inside. Obviously she had not seen him earlier when she ran out of the tent. Just as Mahlah went into the tent, his sisters, the twins, arrived together. Nobody seems to understand how his two sisters had continued to do everything together, including marriage. They were born twins and had remained twined ever since. They had married on the same day. One's family mirrored the other. They had the same number of children, and their husbands were beginning to look like twins themselves. When they were growing up, people had forecast that marriage would be the thing that would help separate them. But that had not been the case; instead they appeared to have gotten closer with marriage. They were identical in looks and were identical in every other way. The two of them were facing him wearing the same expression of concern. He could not find his voice, so he just motioned for them to go into his tent where they were likely to get all the answers to their questions. His focus was praying that his son would survive.

This year as part of his pledge to secure his son, he'd planned to release Kish earlier than the law stipulated. The little slave boy was almost sixteen. He was less diffident, more sociable. He had accepted Zelophehad as a part of his life, learning from him like a son would. He cherished his relationship with Kish, even though he was his slave. He was learning valuable lessons about growing up as a boy today, which outmoded his own experience with his father. Their situation was not too different. He had grown up in Egypt during their oppression under Pharaoh. He had watched as his father and his uncles had worked and lived in a hostile environment in Egypt. But he had happy childhood memories, growing up in Goshen. His father as well as many Israelite fathers had been resolute in training their young males in such a way that they stood shoulder to shoulder with their Egyptian counterparts, if not a head taller. Where the Egyptian boys were taught modern arts, they had been taught skills. Where they were taught to rule, they had been taught to stoop to conquer. Where the Egyptian boys were confused with many gods, they had been taught about a Superior God, who chose them from among all the nations as his special people. So he had grown up confident, never feeling inferior to any Egyptian boy his age. But through Kish he'd learned that many boys his age whether free or not were governed by fears and uncertainties. They were unsure of tomorrow. Kish told him that they could not dream in the wilderness. Kish had confided in him that he dreamed of leaving the camp someday for a surer lifestyle. As much as he was saddened by Kish's revelation, he knew all hope was not lost with this generation having had the privilege of relating also with his nephews. From them he'd also gleaned priceless information. They were different from his generation. They were bold, adventurous and eager to get to the promised land. Even though they did not see most of the miraculous acts they had witnessed, they believed more than his generation. He had come to the conclusion that there were two groups of this generation. The ones who felt helpless and hopeless like Kish because of their present circumstance. The other group on the other hand were set for tomorrow. He was thankful that his nephews belonged to the later group. He resolved the more to set Kish free in the later part of the year, hoping that would change him to thinking more like his nephews.

# 7

THE FOLLOWING DAY THINGS had calmed down and Zelophehad was hopeful again. The bleeding had stopped and the pains were much less thanks to some concoction the midwife had administered to his wife. She had advised his wife to remain lying down for several days, no activity whatsoever. The midwife had also commended his Mahlah for the role that she had played. The reclined position she'd placed her mother in and the back rubs she had given apparently had been just the right things to do. Zelophehad was proud of his daughter. He remembered that Miriam the prophetess had been a midwife herself at a very young age. She had also helped her mother save Moses from Pharaoh's death decree. He felt quite accomplished with his eldest daughter who seemed to be fulfilling his desire of her and her sisters becoming like Miriam. He was smiling at this realization until as he remembered his Mahlah was fast becoming a woman as she was due for Bat Mitzvah soon. Life as a woman was very different from the protected life of a girl. He could not imagine his little Mahlah taken away from him to answer to some other man. He shuddered as he thought of her bearing children as her mother was now. She was almost fourteen, which meant that in a couple of years his nightmares might become reality. He got some little comfort remembering that their women were strong when it came to childbirth. You could find them working in the fields till very late pregnancy. At delivery, they endured labor pains like you would a headache and delivery was pretty fast for them. This very fact had frustrated the Egyptians when they sought to subdue them by killing all their newborns. The midwives were nearly useless to Pharaoh because the Hebrew women had their babies before the midwives could get to them. Mahlah was as much a Hebrew woman, so he would not worry much about this. He has seen his wife live up to that standard with all his four daughters. The only time he'd ever had to worry was with the early phase of her first pregnancy until now. He reckoned that his wife must have been in serious pains yesterday because he'd been around her in all four deliveries and never heard her cry the way she did. He was still concerned, his imagination set wild by his wife's description of the pain. She had described to him that the pains were like stabs with a knife. He was suspicious that some evil spirit was responsible, seeing that the baby in his wife's womb was the son he has desired for so long. He had repented from going to a diviner and given a guilt offering, so it could not be his judgment. Could it be what Helon said was true. His friend Helon had suggested that every now and then evil spirits played such games. He said they had the ability to see the star of an unborn child and if destined for greatness, would attempt to kill that child in the womb. He shivered as he felt cold suddenly and shrugged his shoulder. He should speak to Aaron the high priest about this, but just as he thought of that, he squelched the thought. The thought of how he would present this matter and not be found guilty of something he could not put a finger on. There were serious instructions given to them to keep away from the esoteric, invisible realm. They were to concern themselves only with that which is revealed and revealed only through Moses and the high priest. Witchcraft, divination, fortune telling, and like practices were forbidden among them. He would just have to figure this one out by himself. It might also do him good to stay away from Helon and his stories for now, he decided.

Zelophehad went into the tent to check on his wife. His daughters were such great helps. They had taken over the tent, making sure it was clean and tidy and that their mother was comfortable. His sister had offered to prepare meals for his family for as long as his wife was confined to bed rest. "How are my women doing?" "Very well father," Mahlah and Noah replied in unison, and their mother smiled. His wife looked better but was still wincing every now and then. She was in the fifth month of her pregnancy, but he wished they could enter the ninth month right away and be over with all the anxieties. Everyone was concerned about his wife, even his mother. She had been up all night praying and today he learned that she was on a fast. He looked across the room, catching his mother's worried gaze and mouthed, "Thank you, Imah." He had come to note that he got along better with his mother in crises. He enjoyed times like this when his family came together in support of one another but wished that they did not have to wait for crises to do so. He turned back his gaze to his wife and daughters, asking if they had eaten supper. "No father, we were waiting for you to return," Mahlah responded as she made her way to the cooking area. They always broke bread together in the evening as was the tradition for every Israelite family. It was more than a family eating together. It was more of a feast of remembrance as the fathers told stories of their dealings with YHWH. Here children were taught about the Lord and the Lord's people. They were taught their origins, their patriarchs, their deliverance, the promised land, the law and ordinances in bits. "Did you prepare all these by yourself?" he asked Mahlah as they all sat around the mat of food she presented. It was the whole thigh of a young goat cooked in its milk. There was a bowl of bitter herbs he loved so much and coriander bread to accompany it. Their meals were simple. They baked or boiled manna for breakfast. They ate broth and soups for lunch and snacked on grasshoppers, locusts, and crickets. For supper they ate meat of any animal with divided, cloven hooves that chewed the cud. Every now and then as the season permitted they substituted the herbivores with scaled fishes or birds like pigeons, quails, and doves. YHWH had once rained down the most delicious quails on them for forty days in the desert of Sin. Now they could only find them by hunting for them during the cold seasons. They had more than enough to eat now, especially as they now had long stays at their camps. They planted olives, grapes, and grains of all sorts. They did not depend only on the manna which still rained faithfully every morning. His own focus in the last seven years had been olive groves. It was easier than keeping a vineyard and more profitable, the pressed oil serving as fuel, cooking oil and as emollients for some skin conditions.

He blessed the meal set before him and he blessed his family, calling everyone's name one by one in prayer. This time he surprised his entire family by including "little Hepher." They forgot to respond, all taken aback especially his wife and mother until Milcah, who was just beginning to speak, said, "Aah-men." They all erupted in laughter, defusing the tension in the air.

## 8

ZELOPHEHAD FELT TIRED AND looked tired and he knew it was not mere physical fatigue but more to do with his state of mind. His heart was heavy. Tirzah, his energetic and very interesting child, was a girl, not the son he had anticipated. They were still in the desert of Paran. There had not been any more missions again to Canaan as he had expected five years ago. Last month his uncle Gamaliel, who was their head, had called an assembly of the Manasseh tribe. It was warnings galore. Apparently some Israelite men were crossing boundaries they were not supposed to. Consequently they were facing a lot of difficult cases that the elders could not deal with. One of their men years back had kidnapped a Jebusite woman, who he married contrary to their law. The couple had produced a son and now that son was a menace in the camp. He killed another man in anger and when he was brought to book, his mother called on her relatives, the Jebusites, for revenge. The Jebusites, like the Hivitites, Amorites, and Amalekites, looked for every opportunity to attack them. They were bracing for another war and there was a lot of tension in their camp. Now he had not just his failure to produce a son to worry about, but he was also worried about keeping his family safe and making it to the promised land. He looked across the field to see his wife and five daughters happily talking and laughing as they were working on his field. The image he would have preferred was that of sons running on that field showing off their military skills, like he and his brothers used to do. It was the second day of the month of Nissan and there was a lot of excitement in the air also. Despite the heaviness he felt he could not help but look forward to Pesach. Pesach, the celebration of the Passover, would begin on the fifteenth day of the month and would last seven to eight days. He worried a little about the four days of mandatory holiday that would prevent him from catching up on his pile of work. He'd just acquired another field on a fertile hillside. He wanted to dig it up, clear up stones, and plant some vines since no one knew when their next move would be. Every time he thought of physical work it constantly reminded him of his lack of sons to lighten his physical burden. Kish had disappeared the moment he got his freedom two years ago amidst so many ruckuses. Kish had failed him just as Tirzah failed to be born his long-anticipated son. He had wanted Kish to stay and be a part of his household, in the absence of a son. But the ingrate had not only gotten in trouble but put him right in the deep of that trouble. He had stolen a ewe from his former master, in hope of getting some shekels to redeem his mother and sister. As always, Zelophehad had been shackled with the responsibility of a restitution to save the boy from being sold into slavery again. He had scolded Kish so severely and by the next day he had disappeared never to return. He still prayed every now and then that he would remain safe. His wife and daughters were very hardworking and helpful. They did a lot more than other females he knew around their camp. However it was nothing like having young sturdy men working your field, like Baruch's sons did. They always got everything done on time. Early last year they had had a storm with strong winds that had brought down most of their tents. He remembered how he had struggled with the girls to hold up their collapsing tent. Fearing for their safety, he had called out to his brother Baruch. But because they had also been affected by the storm they had not been able to help until much later. His tent had been one of the last ones to get back up. With all the trouble they had had lately, Pesach would definitely be a very welcome change. There had been a lot of deaths lately in the camp, almost equaling the one that followed their rebellion after the mission to Canaan. Every person who had participated in that rebellion were gone. In addition, thousands of the people who against Moses' advice went up against the Amalekites in bid to make amends for their disobedience, had died at the hands of the Amalekites in Hormah. Even though it had been almost thirty years since that had happened, it looked like they were being downsized or sorted out in fulfillment of the prophecy that had followed the rebellion. YHWH had sworn that none of the people who had taken part in that rebellion would make it to the promised land. He was grateful to his wife, who had prevented him from joining that protest thirty years ago. This time around he was not exempted from the devastation of death. His friend Helon and his twenty-two-year-old son died from a strange accident last year. Two months after losing his best friend he lost one of his brothers just as he was recovering from that grief. He tried to shake off his feelings of sadness and weariness, and was grateful for the call for the twelfth-hour prayer. At least, he thought to himself, "If nothing else, prayer should refresh my soul and spirit." He got up from under the shady sycamore tree and began to walk toward the camp. His wife fell in step with him as he walked toward their tent. He collected her heavy basket so it would not slow them down. He looked behind at Mahlah, who was carrying her baby sister Tirzah, their fifth daughter, and likely their last issue, because of what had happened during her birth. Mahlah was old enough for full participation in every religious activity now that they had celebrated her Bat Mitzvah. In a few months Noah and Hoglah would also qualify. He guessed he should be counting his blessings rather than his losses. The girls were like sponges, absorbing everything he and his wife were teaching them. At the last Pesach, Mahlah had been allowed to join her mother and the women who sang and played timbrels with the prophetess Miriam leading. Zelophehad believed that someday it would be his Mahlah in the place of Miriam leading the women in songs. "We must all remember to pray for Mother that YHWH will strengthen her body and help her get over her grief," his wife said. "Well, also remember to pray that she would stop making my life miserable, too, I also lost a brother and my best friend," Zelophehad said with irritation and looked back just in time to catch Mahlah smiling while his wife frowned. His Mahlah was more like him. She was his daughter through and through. She was not afraid of him, unlike Noah. She was always bold to approach him when no one could. "Did you tell Noah what to do with the rest of the olives?" he asked his wife. As if she could read his mind, she began a long tirade, telling him that Noah was very capable and indirectly scolded him for showing preference for Mahlah all the time. "Woman, I only asked a question of concern. I appreciate what you are doing with our girls and I love them all." "Well then, thank you, my lord," she retorted, and he smiled.

# 9

THIS YEAR'S MONTH OF Nissan was in mid-summer unlike last year's, which had been in late spring. It was the morning of the fourteenth day of Nissan. The sun was already high and there was a lot of excitement in the camp. Pesach was to begin tonight. They all had today as the last day to get rid of every leavened bread—chametz—and all the firstborn males were to begin a fast tonight. Zelophehad felt his stomach grumble as he remembered the fast and he rolled his eyes. It was going to be a very hot day. He prayed he would survive it. The celebration of the Passover was a big deal for them all. It was a major festival to commemorate their deliverance from Egypt. As a law, they were to celebrate their deliverance every year. The celebration would last for seven full days, and during this period all they were to eat was unleavened bread—matzah. No work whatsoever on the first two days and the last two days. At twilight he was going to slaughter a lamb for his family, mark his tent with the blood of the lamb, and they would gather together to roast and eat the lamb with bitter herbs. Before he had his daughters, when it was only him and his wife, they used to do this with his parents and his siblings. But now the Hepherite clan had expanded. All his siblings had enough numbers in their families to do their own thing. Small families of less than three would merge together tonight to eat the Passover feast. Before the meal at twilight they would hold a sacred assembly, and every family was to present themselves at the tent of meeting. Moses, Aaron, and the Levites would have their hands full today ministering to over six hundred thousand of them and he thanked the Lord that they were very capable. He always looked forward to the prophetess Miriam's ministration. She was a remarkable woman. She had such oratory prowess, which exceeded even Aaron's. On the last day of Pesach, the seventh day, she always lead the women in songs and dance at the climax of the celebration. And what was more, she had taken note of his Mahlah during last year's celebration. She'd commented on how talented his Mahlah was. As Zelophehad remembered this he smiled sheepishly and felt that he had proved a point to his mother. None of his nephews had gotten any such attention, at least not from the number one woman in their nation. His brother Baruch approached him just then and asked why he was smiling. He'd been so absorbed with his thoughts that he had not heard his daughter usher Baruch into their tent. "Never mind that," he said nonchalantly. He could not afford his brother condemning him for vanity. And he would not stop taking pride in his Mahlah even for the littlest things. Baruch had come to find out if there was anything he could do to help him for the day, knowing that he was doing the firstborn fast. He was grateful for his brother's thoughtfulness. He patted him on the shoulder and jokingly said, "Give me two of your sons for two of my girls," and they both erupted into laughter. It was their private joke and he dared not say this in his wife's hearing. "Tell me, is it true what I hear about another possible uprising in the camp, what is going on?" Zelophehad asked his brother, who appeared to always keep his ears to the ground. He told him that a group of people led by Korah, a Levite, and two Reubenites were planning to challenge Moses on the issue of who qualified and who did not qualify to enter the tabernacle. Zelophehad got angry, irritated, and disgusted all at the same time. He exploded, "When will these people learn their lessons and stop incurring the wrath of YHWH. They should know by now that Moses does nothing except what YHWH directs him to do. How dare they question his authority?" Looking at him with admiration, his brother said, "Well, we hope they do not carry through with it. For now it is just a rumor and you know what! I used to worry about you getting into such groups but I have noticed you are different now since you lost your friend Helon." "One cannot be a fool forever. We are supposed to learn from the mistakes of others and not repeat them," Zelophehad replied. His brother hurried off and left him thinking about those mistakes. One of such had been the golden calf. It had been a shameful and regrettable event that has cost him and all firstborns their lot. All the firstborn were originally intended to serve as priests and temple functionaries of Israel. However, after that particular mistake, the tribe of Levi had been chosen over the firstborn for this sacred role because they were the only ones who had not participated in that abominable act. He knew that he would have been more relevant in their community, son or no son, had that not happened.

They were celebrating the second day of Pesach, on the fifteenth day of the month of Nissan, and already an offender had been caught. A man from the tribe of Naphthali was caught working. Zelophehad wondered how he had managed to get himself caught, poor, unfortunate man. Every now and then they were all guilty of doing some form of work on the Sabbath, but the point was, you don't get caught. His friend Helon had always said that he suspected the reason for the many sin and guilt offerings on Yom Sheini, the day after Sabbath was because of this very thing. The Napthali caught was to be stoned to death after Pesach, and Zelophehad felt sorry for him and his family. The truth was that no one was infallible. He could remember occasions when unknowingly on Sabbaths he found himself doing something that may have been regarded as work had he been seen or caught by witnesses. He turned his mind away from the sorry story and began to think of ways to make the days more exciting for his family as they continued the celebration of Pesach. He was glad his mother was in a better mood since the beginning of the week. Whether it was his wife's prayers or just the excitement in the air, he was grateful for respite from her sour comments anyhow. They would again eat unleavened bread made from manna tonight. Since the beginning of Pesach, the women had to collect more omers of manna to enable them make unleavened bread, which was more difficult to make than chatmetz. He was watching his wife and Mahlah kneading some more matzahs. "Father would you go and watch the stoning?" Noah asked him. "No I rather watch your mother prepare our meal instead." His daughters found that amusing and began to laugh, not truly understanding the implication of someone being stoned. "Hoglah, come over here and turn the stove down for me. Noah, come and join Mahlah in kneading this dough like I taught you," his wife commanded her daughters like a captain, obviously not in support of their amusement. "You do not laugh at such matters, you hear me. No one deserves to die such a horrible death. What we do is to pray that the family of this man will not be overwhelmed with grief." Hoglah, who was fast becoming an advocate, always having something to say in defense of her sisters and herself, responded defensively. "Imah, we were only laughing at father, not the offender." "I have told you, young lady, that you do not talk back when I make a correction. You should all know when a situation is grim and when you can afford to laugh." Hoglah nodded in obedience and bent over the stove to pull out some more wood, as instructed by her mother. "Milcah, you are making too much noise, keep it down," Hoglah said irritably as she left the cooking area to find a spot far across the room to lick her wounds. Milcah was running around the room trying to catch their baby sister, Tirzah, who was making so much noise. Zelophehad continued to watch his household as they each continued to display their peculiarities. Tirzah was only three but he could see her character already being formed. She was very strong willed and determined, like her grandmother. Her two older sisters were trying to keep her away from the area of the floor set with mats, candle holders, and utensils for their Passover meal. But there she kept going. He glanced at his mother in her corner looking very peaceful and happy with herself. She looked like a domesticated cat that was well taken care of. He felt he should cut her some slack. His mother was old and life had not been too pleasant to her either. She had been an independent woman running her own space and husband until his father had died rather too early. According to their customs she could not continue to live alone, so she moved in with him since he was the firstborn. She tried to run him and his home, but he would not stand for any of it. They quarreled all the time and then made up, thanks to his wife, who was a real peacemaker. He hoped she would make it to the promised land. This was their twenty-eighth year of celebrating Pesach since they had left Egypt. And every year they concluded the celebration with the same statement: "May we celebrate Pesach next year in the promised land."

# 10

Zelophehad stood beside his brother Baruch at their tribal assembly, not liking what he was hearing. There had been a solemn meeting among the tribal heads, the council, and the spiritual leaders last night. Today his uncle Gamaliel, their head, was addressing all the men from the age of twenty upward. They were going to intensify their military training as ordered by Moses. Their renowned enemies, the Amalekites, were planning to attack in retaliation for what happened at Hormah over thirty years ago. After the mission to Canaan, a group of their soldiers had attacked the hill country without consent from Moses. They had meant it as an act of repentance after their rebellion. Their act of bravery had backfired, with the Amalekites killing many and chasing them to Hormah. Helpless, they had pleaded for help from Moses, who had intervened, and they had won that battle at Hormah. He was not too surprised at this latest development. He has been living in trepidation lately as one issue after the other kept cropping up, including the death of his mother. He just wanted this journey to be over with. This intensification in training would mean less time with their families and work. Zelophehad was a strong man and a soldier equal to the task, as they all were, but right now he felt too old and tired for any war. He wanted to spend more time with his family at this stage that his girls were fast becoming women. He wanted to protect them. Mahlah and Noah were in their early twenties. Hoglah was nineteen, Milcah was fourteen, and his baby Tirzah was eleven preparing for Bat Mitzvah. He looked at his brother Baruch with concern. If they had to go to war, it would mean his whole house. He had three sons who were of age and trained soldiers. "What about those of us still in mourning, would we be exempted?" his brother asked. "I am aware of that, Ben Hepher, but after the thirtieth day, you are all required to report to the training fields." Zelophehad could not believe his mother was gone. It was already thirty days after her burial and yet it felt like just yesterday. He whispered to his brother, "Today marks the thirtieth day." Because she was a third-generation wife of the tribe of Manasseh, her burial had been a big affair. Her death had brought together almost the whole tribe. He got to know second and third cousins and a lot of the fifth generation with his mother's passing. He was amazed at how much they had grown as a tribe. They used to be the smallest tribe when they were in Egypt, but he understood that the last census showed they had quadrupled in size.

There was so much noise as thousands of them returned to their tents after the meeting. Their organization was quite remarkableand was reflected in the way the herd of people separated into groups of hundreds, and then into groups of tens, as they made their way home. The Hepher clan was about seventy, and he was the head by virtue of birth. As he and his brother Baruch walked back to their tents, Zelophehad noticed his brother was looking unusually worried and he knew it was not just about the loss of their mother and the news of impending war. "What is happening with you? Are you going to divorce her?" A couple of years ago Baruch, against Zelophehad's counsel, had taken a second wife who was as young as his second son. Now it appeared what he feared was already in motion. Several people have reported to Baruch on his young wife's clandestine affairs. Though it was a disgrace for their family, his advice was for Baruch to let her go, but he was insisting on taking her to the priest for the test for unfaithfulness. "Look Baruch, do not let jealousy cloud your judgment. If you take her to the priest, she will end off worse. You know that she is guilty and a curse will be put on her. Not as if she does not deserve it for disgracing this family." "Hmm, I never said that she is guilty," Baruch retorted. "Well with every indication and evidence, she is guilty. You are only denying it because of your pride and I will not talk to you about this again. I wash my hands off," Zelophehad concluded, not wanting to continue this particular topic.

He had too much on his hands anyway to be bothered about his brother's family affairs. When Baruch had wanted to take that young lady as wife, he and their mother had advised against it. For the first time he and his mother agreed about something even though she had spoiled that little gratification by insinuating that Zelophehad was the one in need of another wife. He must stop thinking about the bad and think good of his mother now she was gone. He walked past his tent and went toward his grain field. His wife and daughters were there as he expected. His daughters were growing quickly into beautiful women. He watched as a young Benjamite walked past his family and exchanged a look with his fourth daughter, Milcah. "Oh no!" he thought, repulsed. He knew that sooner or later his girls would begin to receive attention from men and would end up wives. With that came the realization that they would all be gone someday and he would have no one to continue his house. He had been so hopeful when his wife had gotten pregnant with their last girl, Tirzah. But his expectations had not been fulfilled. Of all his daughters, Tirzah was the most unusual. She liked everything about the opposite sex and hated everything about her sex, especially the restrictions. No matter how hard his wife tried to make her a lady, she behaved like a boy. His wife felt it was their fault. She felt that somehow they had by some way communicated to Tirzah in the womb how much they had wanted her to be a male. Even though she was the youngest, she was the strongest and bravest. She was stubborn like a mule and strong willed. She frowned on her sisters interest in the opposite sex, called it silliness, and whenever they talked about marriage and things they wanted as women she kept very quiet. You could often find her horning her skills with bows and arrows while her sisters did the cooking and other domestic chores. She had interestingly been her grandmother's favorite. Almost as if she saw her as the grandson she had always wanted from her firstborn. Zelophehad's mother had died after a very crippling disease that affected her lungs. Tirzah had not been afraid like his other daughters to stay close to her grandmother, even when his wife feared her wracking cough could be contagious. And when she passed on, it was Tirzah that had been by her side getting words of blessing from her. He felt a surge of emotions as he looked his daughters over without them being aware of it. They may not be men but they were his jewels. He had taught and trained them to the best of his knowledge. They were strong and courageous women and were well able to measure up to any of their male cousins. He had over the years consistently taught them to think of themselves as equals to any of their male cousins and did not intend to stop, despite his wife's concerns.

## 1 1

Zelophehad held on to his wife's hand and looked around for his daughters as he took his last breaths, but Mahlah was missing. Their lives has been turned upside down in a twinkle of an eye. As he felt weaker and weaker he wished Mahlah would come along before he finally closed his eyes. He eyes grew dimmer and the cries of "Abba…" from his daughters became too faint. It was as if a cold, strong hand was pulling at him. He could no longer feel the pains in his broken limbs, but the excruciating pain with each breath was growing. He stopped breathing when he could no longer bear the pain.

He had turned sixty last year and with that it appeared he had lost his stamina and strength. He found himself putting off a lot of chores and lagging behind on his farm work. Even though the girls were grown, there was a limit to what he would allow them do because they were women. Consequently he had left a large portion of his field unattended to. His uncle Gamaliel had ordered him to give up his field to a cousin belonging to the Helekites clan. He had stubbornly refused. Unfortunately, that cousin had set his eyes on his field and betrayed him when an opportunity had presented itself. He had caught him collecting wood the day before on the Sabbath and cried wolf. He knew he should not have taken that risk, but it had been months since his wife had begged him to fix the rotting stake holding up their tent. But his health had not been the same for some time, even though he denied it several times when his wife confronted him. And so he had woken up this fateful day stronger than he had been in the past days and planned to use that energy quickly before it ebbed away. He had been caught by this cousin who refused to cover him because of his ulterior motives. Everything happened so fast. He had been taken to Moses and the council, who had deliberated on his matter the whole day while he had been kept in custody outside the camp. Finally the verdict was given early the following morning. He had committed an act punishable by death and was stoned.

"My lord, my lord," shouted his wife as she shook his lifeless body. She could not believe her husband was dead just like that. Not an honorable death at war but stoned like a dog. She felt her heart would burst and she was almost losing her mind. Everything else that happened thereafter was unreal to her. Baruch's sons came and took charge, tearing the girls away from their father's limp body. They carried him away from the open field to be embalmed and buried immediately.

Mahlah was so agitated that she could not stand still but walked round and round the same perimeter behind their tent. She cried bitterly as she thought of her father taking his last breaths in pain. She had been in shock and immobilized since the news had gotten to them yesterday. They had all been inside the tent because it was Sabbath, without realizing that their father was absent. She had thought he was getting more rest and did not want to be disturbed until one of Uncle Baruch's sons came with the dreadful news. She had noticed her father had woken up earlier that day stronger than he had been for some time, but she had not expected he would go out to the fields on the Sabbath. Mahlah knew she was in denial. She was trying very hard not to picture her father lying dead. She had been so shocked that she had not been able to go with her mother and sisters to see her father take his last breaths. She let out a scream and tears began to pelt down her face. Why did he have to break the Sabbath just to make them happy? He could have sent her and Tirzah during the week to get the wood. She had insisted on several occasions to do things for him when she had noticed his failing health, but he would not let her. She had argued with him and questioned why he had taken all the time to teach them all the manly things and yet would not allow them to help him. She ran toward the front of their tent as she heard her mother's wailing voice, wondering how their mother would cope. This would surely kill her, Mahlah thought.

Her mother loved and doted on her father. She had been dependent on him all her life. Theirs had been a wonderful marriage despite having no sons. She respected her father for sticking with their mother even when their grandmother had encouraged and pushed for another woman. Oh how she loved her father. But how could he have done this to them. Breaking the Sabbath and getting killed like a dog. Just last week for the first time in her life she had dared to watch the stoning of an offender. She'd been so disturbed afterwards, never imagining that the same fate would befall her own dear father. She wept bitterly as she quickened her steps toward the entrance of their tent. She went straight to her mother and took her in her arms while she sobbed. She took over the situation as was expected of her. She looked around at her sisters who were wailing as much as their mother and decided she would be strong for them.

It was late evening when the wailing simmered down a little. They could not even begin the official mourning until twilight. They were alone, all huddled together with their mother like they used to do when they were younger. They had been crying since morning and their mother refused to be comforted for one moment. All through the day she kept saying it was her fault that her husband went out to fetch wood on a Sabbath day. Mahlah consoled her to no avail. "Mother it was not your fault. It was our fault for not being the sons that he so badly needed." "But I bore you all, so it is my fault that I did not give him sons to lighten his burdens." Hoglah who had been quiet since the news came, hissed and spoke heatedly for the first time. "Quit talking such nonsense. Can't you see what happened to father? He was betrayed by a man who is supposed to be kin just because of greed and envy. If they think they can take over our father's properties because he has no son, they are in for a surprise." Noah, a peacemaker like her mother, quickly intervened with words of comfort and peace. "Hoglah, you are presumptuous. Mother, it is not your fault or anybody's fault. This has happened for a reason we do not yet understand because we are in pain. We need all the support we can get from our people now that father is gone. We are all women and have no say where men speak. Thank the Lord for Uncle Baruch and his sons that we are sure of being there for us. But we need to live peaceably with everyone."

## 12

THEIR FATHER'S BODY WAS buried immediately by his nephews far outside the camp. Mahlah and her mother and sisters had not been permitted to be there. His two sisters had been the ones to prepare his body for burial. Mahlah was grateful that they had been spared that aspect. The official mourning had begun with plenty of well-wishers coming in and out of their tent. It was a miserable time for them all. They sat with relatives, not much talk, just mourning until it was late into the night. Her mother and Noah were still sobbing but she and her other sisters were tearless. She wondered when her mother's tears would end. It was like a dam had broken. In all her life Mahlah had only seen her mother cry twice or so and then never like this. She had cried when she had Tirzah because of the disappointment and the fact that she could not have any more babies. The other time had been when they lost their uncle and their father's best friend simultaneously. She did not even remember her crying when their grandmother had died, and she could not blame her. Her grandmother had been a tough woman. She had not made life easy for their mother and had even transferred some of that animosity toward them, except for Tirzah, who had been her favorite. Family and friends were coming by to sympathize with them and there was a dirge being played as was their custom. She wished the women playing the dirge would stop because it seems to be encouraging her mother to cry the more. She saw her uncle Baruch trying to turn away the children of the cousin who had been responsible for raising the alarm that led to her father's death. How tactless of them. Mahlah saw her mother in the midst of her sobs look in her uncle's direction with a look of gratitude. Thank God Hoglah did not see them for she would have caused a scene no doubt.

Uncle Baruch came over and spoke in her ear. He told her to take her mother inside and make her some chamomile drink to relax her. Baruch was her favorite uncle and relative. And because she had been the closest to her father they were also close. She enjoyed talking to him and getting counsel from him. He was unlike her other male relatives who treated her and her sisters as less than humans just because they were females. She was happy that they at least had him now that their father was gone. His sons were all in the army representing their tribe, and whenever they were not at a war front or at the training camp, they related well with Mahlah and her sisters. They treated them like their sisters. She took her mother behind the curtain that separated the sitting area and their sleeping quarters. The tent felt different all of a sudden, as if aware that the head of the house has departed. It felt funny and she wondered if her mother would be able to sleep alone without her father whom she had been with for almost four decades. When their grandmother had died it had not felt like this even though she had lived with them for as long as she could remember. She laid her mother down and sat beside her, stroking her face and hair, while Noah prepared the herbal drink for her. After the drink, her mother fell asleep almost immediately. She suspected her sister had probably been too generous with the herbs. By the time she got back outside she saw that her uncle had managed to disperse the well-wishers. She was both grateful and relieved. After the last guest left and her sisters retired for the night, she decided to sit out alone for some time, just like her father used to do. She was the eldest of her sisters and naturally would be responsible for a lot of things from now on. That thought dawning made her heart skip a beat. She has never been a fearful or anxious person, especially not with the type of person her father had been. He had prepared her for many things in life except for this. She had never imagined or seen life without him in the picture. All of her life, he has always been around. He did everything for her mother and them, his daughters. She let out a sigh and resolved that her primary responsibility from now on would be to take care of her mother and sisters, just like he had. She knew she and her sisters had all they needed to marry well thanks to their parents, but for the time being they need to survive their father's demise. She was turning twenty five in the month of Kislev, at the end of the year. Her mother had married her father at sixteen, but her father said it was different for her and her sisters. He was not in a hurry to marry them off he'd said. He wanted some semblance of stability as concerning their journey to the promised land. He had married and had them all in the wilderness, but wanted things to be different for them. Her mother said it was fear of letting go and having an empty house. Whatever the case, she vowed to make sure her father's dreams came true. He'd wanted her to be like Miriam. That, she believed, was not in her hands but in the hands of the Lord, who gives gifts and destiny to men. Her concern now was how they were going to be heard as women. How were they going to keep their father's inheritance with all the uncles and cousins so eager to take over? One thing was sure, she needed the Lord now more than ever. She had never been a particularly religious person like her mother. She grew up watching her mother go the extra mile fasting, praying, and giving offerings. She had learned from her mother, though, that the more you seek the Lord the more you were blessed. Somewhere she had heard that he reveals things that are hidden to those who seek him and guides your path so you do not stumble. And he will subdue your enemies. That part she liked the most. Her mother always said she was a thinker like her father, always analyzing things. The moment she thought of him she began sobbing afresh. She was going to miss him sorely. He had been a good father to her and her sisters. Even though she knew how much he wanted a son, he never made her and her sisters feel inadequate in anyway. He had taught them things no father teaches their daughter in Israel. He kept telling them all the time that he did not want them to be cheated in life because they were women. He'd taught them like men. She smiled as she remembered an occasion when a little boy her age had tried to bully her when she was ten. Her father had mischievously encouraged her to fight back instead of separating them, and oh, how she had dealt with the boy putting the fear of her in him for a long time. She smiled as she remembered another occasion when Noah, who was very like their mother, soft and gentle, refused to join them in learning what her father had termed self-defense skills. Her father had pitted wild Tirzah against Noah to prove to her that she needed those skills to defend herself. Tirzah, the baby of the house, had beaten Noah up and they had laughed so hard. He'd brought them up in an unconventional way because he wanted them to be different. Growing up had been fun because of him. She remembered how her friends used to envy the fact that she could do a lot of things most girls in Israel could not do. Even Noah, who was all emotional and girly, had to develop some necessary toughness. Well now they were all trying to be more like ladies thanks to their mother, who thought marriage was next on the agenda. She was grateful to the Lord that she and her sisters were comely to behold. They were all very beautiful in different ways, almost like a compensation for not being males. Mahlah had long dark curly hair and big beautiful brown eyes and was tall and willowy. Noah was red-headed, very fair with green luminous eyes, and was delicately slim. Hoglah was also red-headed with sparkling deep brown eyes that appeared almost black, and she was curvy without being too voluptuous. Milcah had dark exotic looks more like a Cushite, with slanted eyes and full lips. And Tirzah at eleven was already a beauty and it was apparent she would be the tallest of them. She had very long straight black hair and fair skin that had their mother worried all the time, as she loved to roam and wander in the sun unprotected. Tirzah hated the traditional shawl that women wrapped around their head and face. She loved to run and feel the wind in her face. The girls were also talented. Mahlah could sing and play almost any musical instrument. Noah had a voice like a nightingale she inherited from their mother who loved to sing. Noah had also learned from their grandmother to weave goat's hair, special clothing worn by the priests. Hoglah was an excellent perfumer, known all over the camp. She could concoct any fragrance to match the occasion for which it was used. Milcah was good with embroidery on scarlet and fine linens—a trade of their mother for years. Tirzah was yet to discover a talent that was appropriate for a lady, but was good with their herds and could shoot a bow better than many men in the camp. Evidently it should not be difficult for them to find husbands when the time was right. "But first things first!" she said to herself. She started to feel a chill and decided to go inside, wondering if her father's spirit would be visiting tonight like people say after a death like this. Well she was not afraid, and if she could actually see him she would tell him how sorry she was and say her goodbyes.

## 13

MAHLAH WOKE UP SUDDENLY with her heart pounding. She had been in a dream so real it had frightened her. She had dreamed that her father had come to see her and they had sat together outside the tent talking. He had given her several instructions of which she could not remember much, except for the part of fighting for their rights when they get to the promised land. She had asked him if he was happy where he was. He'd said no, and immediately a hand had reached out and pulled him away while he resisted and began screaming, terrified. She'd reached out her hand to help him but could not, and in terror she had woken up. She sat up, said a prayer, and then began to cry until she remembered her mother. Quickly she wiped her tears and went to check on her mother. She must have been more tired than she thought and had slept into late morning as she heard her sisters in the cooking area already. Her sisters must have been out already to collect some manna. They were back to depending more on manna again because they were in the desert of Zin where very little grew. They had left Paran, a region of the northern part of Sinai, south of Canaan, after a very long stay. She looked forward to the day quails would rain from the sky again like the manna they have enjoyed for over three decades. When Israel arrived in the desert of Sinai after escaping from Egypt, there had been a scarcity of meat because they had lost most of their livestock on the journey through the desert. The people had complained bitterly, incurring the wrath of YHWH, and Moses had pleaded for the people. The result was quails for forty days. Her mother said it was one of the greatest miracles of their times. But Mahlah thought her people were rather incorrigible. With all she had heard, she judged them severely as unfaithful. What she would give to see the miracles they saw. Her generation only heard how delicious the quails had been but did not know the taste of it. And she may never see quails rain again from the sky because over the years they have been able to rear more livestock, acquiring some from war spoils. For most of the people, their wealth consisted of their livestock. They had through the years also cultivated lands wherever they settled. In Paran, her father had been able to make great yields from olive groves. As they moved from place to place, the women were constantly discovering interesting herbs and vegetables that added some spice to their diet. Recently they discovered melon and cucumbers like they used to have in Egypt, the very same food they nearly forfeited the promised land for.

Still troubled by her nightmare, she preceded to look for her mother. She got to her mother just as she was coming away from her position of prayer facing toward the direction of the tabernacle. She was looking so different having removed every form of finery, even the signet ring her father had given her. Her mother turned around in fright as she came closer, gasping, "Oh it's you, Mahlah." "Yes, Mother, did you get a good sleep?" In a voice that Mahlah could hardly hear, she replied, "Somewhat, the drink helped." "Can I get you some food?" Mahlah asked, feeling uncomfortable with her mother's very somber mood. Before she could get an answer from her mother, Noah came in with a bowl of soup. "Take that back, Noah, I have no need for food now." Wanting to escape, Mahlah collected the soup bowl. "Let me take that, Noah, stay with Mother please." As she was walking out of the tent, some cousins of her mother walked in crying loudly, "We cannot believe that you are gone, O, Zelophehad. You left these beautiful women of yours. O Death!" Mahlah quickly walked out. She knew this would continue for some time, at least for the remaining days of Shiva. For the next seven days there was no bathing or change of clothes for her, her sisters, and mother. They were in mourning and it was the custom to do nothing but mourn for the seven days of Shiva. Apart from Shiva, they would not participate in any celebration for thirty days after their father's burial. She was sure that as far as her mother was concerned it may very well be for life. Mahlah could only hope that for their sakes she would be strong, they needed her now more than ever. Yesterday the burial had not been much because of the circumstance under which her father had died. A lot of their kinsmen had not participated, so she guessed the next seven days would be pretty busy. She knew she ought to stay back with her family, but she needed fresh air and she did not think she could survive all that wailing. She decided to take a walk and think. Tirzah, seeing her, came and hugged her. Mahlah held her for a while and a tear dropped down her cheek. She whispered in her ear that she was going for a walk. "Can I come with you?" "No, please go stay with Mother."

Noah hurried her mother up, helping her to the sitting area where their well-wishers had gathered. She wondered why Mahlah was not there to receive them. These were relatives from her mother's family that she and sisters were not familiar with, because they rarely visited. Her mother was of the tribe of Asher, and her people camped far from them on the northern part of the camp. Noah hoped when they were all married they would be able to keep close, unlike the common trend. The husbands appeared to completely own their families, while wives were kind of estranged from their own families. Noah did not believe it was intentional though. There was no written code that women were to completely abandon their families, it just happened as part of the marriage act. The man's home became your home. His people became your people, and even his religion became yours. For her part, she would be content to marry a man from her own tribe, period. Noah could not help her tears as her mother began a wrenching sob as she saw her people. They began the prayer by the time two more people joined them, making ten of them. Her uncle Baruch led the prayers again today, and Noah felt his pain as she watched him. He and her father had been the closest of their family of six boys and two girls. Her father was the firstborn and her uncle was the last boy and yet they had found an uncommon bonding. Well, she prayed that that bond would continue now between him and them, the family of his dear brother. Through the corner of her eyes she saw Hoglah, Milcah, and Tirzah on the other side of the tent with their cousins, Baruch's sons. Two of his sons who had buried her father were missing because they were unclean after handling her father's corpse. Missing also were their aunties, because they had been the ones who had embalmed him. She scouted round the room looking for her big sister Mahlah, but she was also missing. Noah was concerned about Mahlah because she had been closest to their father. Of all of them, Mahlah had clearly impressed their father even though she was not a son. The same went for Tirzah, except that she had not been old enough to converse maturely with him like Mahlah. She had never been jealous of this fact, content to be their mother's favorite. She looked at her mother with pity and her heart went all out to her. She was a widow, and widows' lives were not pleasant, especially those without sons. But she resolved in her mind with all the courage she could muster that she would not allow her mother to suffer. "Even if it means that I have to sacrifice my life and happiness, God help me, I will do just that," she vowed under her breath.

## 14

MAHLAH TOOK A WALKING path rarely used by people because she wanted to be alone and think. And moreover, she did not want to be seen, as a lot of her people would think she was disrespectful of her father's death. The grass was greener, and there was more of it, at this time of the year, but it rarely grew taller than the level of her shin. She was glad that wild animals rarely came near their tents. Though every now and then there were incidents where young ones went missing and their carcasses were later discovered. The thought sent a shiver down her spine, increasing her worries for Tirzah, who insisted on roaming around on her own with her catapult and stones. And she was unusually skilled with it for a girl. Her mother said she was the beast their father created. It was a very sunny and hot day so Mahlah raised her hand up to screen her face so she could see ahead. She saw a woman in the distance behind the tents of the Kohathites. She was tall and elegantly dressed. She was looking down deep in thought as Mahlah approached her. It was not until she was within six feet of her that she noticed Mahlah, and when she raised her face, Mahlah was surprised that it was their leader's wife, Zipporah. Mahlah bowed her head and was prepared to make a turn around when she beckoned to Mahlah. "I hear your father died yesterday, sorry about that." Mahlah could only stare, too shy and stunned to speak back. Because of the awe many of the people had for Moses, they naturally saw his wife also as an intimidating figure. Even their sons got a share of this, they were respected by all. Stories her parents had told her came rushing into her mind as she beheld Moses' wife. Moses was not respected only just because he was their leader. Moses was next to YHWH as far as they were concerned. Moses, who went up to the mountain to see God himself, and they knew for certain that he had seen God because when he had returned no one had been able to look into his face. His face had been literally transformed into a ball of blinding white light, such that he had to cover his face with a veil for days. News and stories of Moses were not just localized among them. The surrounding nations heard, too, even though they told it differently. They believed the Israelites had this prophet among them who was a son of the gods and that this was the reason they were unbeatable. The fame of Moses and their nation had foreigners coming to join them, converting to their way of life. There was a report of a woman and her whole family waiting in Canaan to become part of them when they took over the land. This woman had rendered help to the Israelite spies, saving their lives in Canaan, and as a payback they had promised to spare her and her family when they took over Canaan. Mahlah looked at Ziporrah through the corners of her eyes and thought how beautiful she still was, even with age. She had this exotic look you saw with the Cushites. She was tall and slim, with a carriage like a queen. "Even though I did not know him, I believe your father was a good man and a good father to you. I have watched your family for some time and watched you girls grow. You and your sisters remind me of my childhood and life with my family in Midian. My father—I am sure you do not know him, but your mother should—had only daughters, seven of us! And I remember the things we had to face as females in Midian just like you have here. We would go to wells to fetch water and would have to wait until all the men were through, even if they came after we did. It was on one such occasion that I met my husband. We were at a well as usual, trying to fetch water and give a drink to our flock of sheep, when some men came along. They tried to bully us out of our turn as usual, but Moses came gallantly to our rescue. I fell in love the moment I saw him, for he was so handsome and regal, a true prince. I thought he was an Egyptian prince." She paused and smiled while Mahlah got rather uncomfortable hearing about this very human side of Moses she had never heard of. "We had good times in Midian, that's where we had our first son, Gershom. I was so happy until unexpectedly Moses changed. He had an encounter with . . ." She looked up to the sky at this point and Mahlah could see tears in her eyes. She swallowed hard and continued. "Well I had thought we will continue our lives in Midian. We were doing well and were very happy. Foolish of me, I guess I miss my family. You must be strong and look after your mother and sisters. It's a good thing your—I mean, our—people do not marry foreign men as such, but be careful that nothing takes you too far from your family." Mahlah nodded and gave her a grateful smile. She watched her take her leave and then let out a pent-up breath. After such an encounter, she decided to go right back to their tent and see how her mother was holding up. She felt some peace and was surprised that Zipporah took notice of them over the years and that they reminded her of her own family. Having something in common with Moses' wife was a gift to her because all her life she had admired Zipporah. But she was piqued by the sadness she'd seen in her eyes. Why was she unhappy, married to such a great man as Moses? She needed more answers other than her missing Midian.

She could not wait to tell her sisters and her mother about this encounter with Zipporah. She had felt her sadness and wondered how long she had been like that. She had thought things were just perfect in her world, being the wife of the most respected man in the whole camp. She thought of the rumors of her strained relationship with her sister-in-law Miriam, the prophetess. At one point, Miriam had made Zipporah the bone of contention between herself and Moses, accusing Moses of having a foreign wife. Zipporah herself apparently had not helped matters, for rumors had it that she had resisted her husband for a long time over the circumcision of their sons. She'd found it very repulsive just like other surrounding nations. It was known that the Cushites condescendingly referred to Hebrew men as—*bridegroom of blood.* Circumcision was the very basis of their identity as the people of God. It began with their forefather Abraham, and God had made it a law for them. Every Israelite male child was to be circumcised on the eighth day of life. Even for the foreigners amongst them, the only way they could become part of them was through circumcision. So Mahlah wondered how she could have contested that. Even if anyone could escape circumcision, which was not even possible, certainly not the sons of the one that God entrusted the very law to. Every law and ordinance they received from YHWH came through Moses.

It was the third morning after her father's burial and Mahlah had the same dream again. She wanted to tell her mother about her dreams but decided against it, as it might further upset her. She got up from her sleeping pallet and decided to go get some food before their relatives, friends, or neighbors started pouring in. While serving herself from the cooking area, she hinted to her sisters of her encounter with Zipporah and got some excitement from all except for Noah. Noah was upset with her for going off and leaving them to attend to all the visitors yesterday. "They all kept asking for you and Uncle Baruch wanted to see you. But no, you must always do it your way." "I am sorry I needed that time to myself and I feel better now," she responded to Noah's outburst with guilt. Noah was sounding like their mother and it looked like she was beginning to play her role too. "Well I am glad you feel better." They all chuckled when Mahlah said, "Yes, Imah." Still feeling a little guilty that she'd abandoned them yesterday, she took charge, wanting to remind her sisters that she was the eldest. "Noah, let's go in and see to mother. The rest of you stay put, no one is to leave the tent today," Mahlah said, looking pointedly at Tirzah. When they got to their mother, Mahlah went to put her arms around her, but without a word her mother shook her off. "Mother, I understand this must be difficult for you, but it is also hard for us and we need you to be strong." But her mother was not in the mood to be comforted. She was stooped over and appeared to be saying something under her breath—maybe prayers. Mahlah felt a little hurt that her mother was not responding to her. "Well I better let you take over, Noah." Noah was the closest to their mother, something they believed was divinely orchestrated. Not only was she close but she shared a lot of her mother's characteristics. She had her looks, her walk, her manners and nature. She could always second guess their mother, which used to tick them off, and at the same time they took advantage of it to manipulate their mother. Noah touched her mother's arm tenderly as she sat beside her. "Mother, I brought you some broth just the way you like it." Noah held up the bowl of broth, praying that she would eat some. In just three days, their mother was looking older. Her parents' relationship had been different from the ones that she knew were common with their people. Her mother had been close to her father in a very special way. They had had mutual respect for each other and were truly friends first, before being man and wife. Noah hoped someday she, too, would find a man in Israel that would treat her the way her father had treated her mother. But for now, her concern was how to get her mother through this.

## 15

It was the month of Tebeth, six months after the demise of their father. There was so much loneliness in their family, not just because their father was no longer there, but more because their mother, though not dead, chose to live like the dead. Their mother was not only mourning but was slowly dying of a broken heart. There was nothing the girls could do to cheer her up or get her off her sleeping pallet or her praying mat. Mahlah felt she could count the number of words she has spoken to them in the last six months. She barely ate and had become so gaunt and old that she looked like death. Two months ago Mahlah had gone to her mother's family in an attempt to help her mother out of this abyss. Their maternal grandmother had spent two months with them but it did not work and so she left. Mahlah's friend Eliana had told her it was a spirit that had possessed her mother and that they needed a spiritualist to deal with it, but Mahlah would not hear of any of that nonsense. She had been taught well enough by her mother that doing any such thing was idolatry, unfaithfulness to God. She could only pray for her mother. She knew her mother still prayed, as was her habit, but she was concerned about what she may be praying for. She suspected she was asking to join her husband in death from every indication. Tirzah, the other day, had gone missing, and Mahlah had thought that will get some reaction from their mother, but surprisingly she had not bulged. Noah, who was her closest and favorite, had not been able to get through to her, either, except for getting her to eat something every now and then. Her uncles and cousins had held a meeting the other day to decide her mother's plight and theirs. They had suggested that the next best thing was for the girls to be married off, but because they did not know what to do with their mother, they had agreed to Uncle Baruch's suggestion to leave them alone. Uncle Baruch had offered to continue to oversee his brother's family, and they had conceded to him since they all knew he was the closest to their father. If they were not in the picture, one of their uncles by the law would have had to take their mother in as wife. She was glad that they had also decided to leave the issue of her father's property for now except for the grain field on the hillside. The head of their tribe, Gamaliel, had still gone ahead and relocated it to a cousin of her father's. None of her father's brothers had wanted it, and they being women could not cultivate the land alone. With Uncle Baruch's help she had been able to take charge of their home. When Tirzah had gone missing it was Uncle Baruch and his sons who went on a search party. She and her sisters had all been so scared not knowing what to do. Tirzah was used to roaming off, away from the camp on her own. That fateful day it turned out that she had out of curiosity decided to go farther into the surrounding wilderness. Armed with her catapult and sling she wandered off and came across a wild cat. She told them she had followed it to its lair and found that they were many more of its kind. So she hid in a tree to watch them but after a while she witnessed something gruesome. She saw them pin down a deer and tear it to pieces for food and she got so terrified that she could not come down from the tree. She had remained in the tree too afraid to do anything until she heard voices calling her name. She had been rescued by her favorite uncle and his sons. Mahlah had scolded her heavily and Noah had begged her with tears never to repeat that. She only hoped that she understood how close she had come to being eaten by those wild cats and was scared enough not to repeat it. She had thought the event would shake their mother out of her world of anesthesia but it had not.

 Ever since her conversation with Zipporrah when her father died, Mahlah has been looking for another opportunity to speak with her again especially as her mother was not talking anymore to her. She missed that motherly encouragement that used to come from every spoken word of wisdom. And another part of her also wanted answers to a lot of questions related to Zipporah. Her friend Eliana had told her that there was a time that Moses sent Zipporrah away to Midian because of some serious disagreement. She also said had if it not been for her father Jethro, who brought her back to the camp with her sons, Zipporah would have been history. Mahlah remembered Zipporah saying it had been love at first sight when she met Moses and was curious about what went wrong. Her own mother had always told her there was much more to marriage than falling in love but she wanted to hear from Zipporah what had really happened to that love. She did not trust what Eliana had told her. Her mother's marriage to her father had been an arranged one and no such story as falling in love at first sight. Her mother said she had prayed about marriage beforehand from the moment she became a Bat Mitzvah. And it seems her prayers had been answered because she did have a wonderful marriage with their father. YHWH granted her so much favor with their father that even when her in-laws would have him take another wife he did not. Polygamy was accepted with their people but it was not common. Most men only resorted to it when their first marriage did not give them their expected desires or fulfillment. Her uncle Baruch had taken another wife because his first wife became an invalid. Unfortunately for him his second wife had been a disgrace. She had defiled their marriage by an amorous affair with another man. She was taken to the priest for a test of unfaithfulness and she failed. The curse had been immediate as they watched her abdomen begin to swell the day after. Mahlah wanted excitement and romance like what Zipporah had with Moses, but she also wanted what her parents had. She had asked her sisters the other day about their expectations for marriage. Noah and Hoglah had surprised her. Noah said she would be fine with their mother or uncle choosing a husband for her and she believed it would work just like their parent's. Hoglah, on the other hand, admitted there was a Benjamite she was in love with and she was waiting for him to propose after Mahlah and Noah were married, as was their custom. Mahlah had told them her plan to stay unmarried until they got to Canaan and were settled. Hoglah had disapproved, saying she wanted to marry soon. After much argument to and fro, she'd resigned with her opinion. She only prayed that they will have that luxury of getting to Canaan first without any interference from their relatives. For now she has to lead her sisters to secure their father's name in Israel.

## 16

Two years after their father's death, their lives still did not appear to have changed much or to have progressed. Their mother was but a shadow of her old self. She lived like an invalid. She did not get around much. Her world consisted only of the perimeters of their tent. Mahlah had been forced to take up much more responsibility than she'd bargained for. They'd lost their grain field to their father's cousin but had done well with rearing herds of sheep and goats even as females. They had tried to fight for their grain field but had not succeeded. They had gone to the council of elders that oversee their tribe but the only support they had gotten was from their uncle Baruch who was now a member of the council. Mahlah had wanted to take it further but her uncle had convinced her to let it go. She had been deviously glad when the camp disembarked shortly after and they had moved to Kadesh Barnea.

She and her sisters were at a well watering their flock when Eliana came with the news that the prophetess Miriam had just died. Too stunned, she refused to believe her until she heard the trumpet, calling for an assembly. They all ran toward their tent to get their shawls and move with the mob of people toward the tent of meeting. Even though they all knew that the prophetess was not young in age, it was still shocking that she had died. Miriam had been a very important figure in the camp. She was the third in position next to Moses and Aaron, the only woman in such a position. Miriam, who all the women looked up to, was gone. Memories of who she had been and all that she had done came rushing to her mind. Mother had told them how she had always stood by her brother Moses since he was born. But as much as she loved and supported her brother Moses, it had not stopped her from confronting him at Hazeroth. Shortly after they had left Egypt, Miriam had a serious quarrel with Moses that nearly cost her life. Always having had an influence over Aaron she had led him to confront Moses. They had questioned and objected to Moses' leadership for no apparent reason other than envy. Miriam had even publicly objected to Moses' wife Zipporah, whom she never liked because she was not an Israelite. Of course the part about her not liking Zipporah was mere speculation, but it was clear that Miriam and Aaron had been jealous of Moses special relationship with the Lord and his prophetic gifts. YHWH had defended Moses and punished Miriam by afflicting her with leprosy, but Moses had pleaded on her behalf and she had been cured after seven days of the worst kind of disgrace.

By the time she and her sisters got to the assembly there was such a racket with thousands of people wailing. It was amazing how organized this large assembly was. They all fell automatically into positions predetermined by the tribes they belonged to. Their clan, the tribe of Manasseh, was at the rear next to the tribe of Ephraim. Prayers were being offered by the high priest Aaron as his sons supported him physically. He was so shaken. It was common knowledge that Aaron and Miriam were very close, having just three years between them in age. People mourned greatly as was expected for a great personality as Miriam. Miriam had very early in life taken up the role of leadership. At the age of seven she prophesied the birth of Moses to her parents Jochebed and Amram. She was there when Moses was discovered in the Nile River by Pharaoh's daughter. She had not been afraid to approach Pharaoh's daughter and cleverly recommend her mother Jochebed as a wet nurse. Above all she was a powerful worshipper. She always led the women in worship, singing and playing timbrels. She would be greatly missed. They did not tell their mother about this sad news before they left for the assembly, but Mahlah was sure that by now Tirzah would have told her. She wondered what her reaction would be, probably not much. They all knew how much her mother admired the prophetess but she was skeptical that even that would elicit any emotions from her mother. She was beginning to give up on her mother, but Noah kept encouraging them all. After two years of hoping, Mahlah was tired. She was glad that she had told Tirzah to stay behind with their mother after leading the herd home. They were going to be here for seven days or longer mourning the prophetess Miriam.

# 17

It was the thirty-eighth year of their journey in the desert in quest for the promised land. Mahlah mused about this journey that had begun long before she and her sisters were born. Their father who had started this journey like many of his generation was out of the race. It was her generation who were not there when this race began that were faced with completing the race and inheriting the promised land. After a long mourning period for the prophetess Miriam they were on the move again, heading for a place near the territory of the Edomites. From what she gathered, her people were happy because they knew they would get help from the Edomites, who were related to the Israelites by their common ancestor Isaac. Everyone was tired of facing enemies all the time. An ally would definitely be a welcome change. So far the only people that had shown the Israelites some corporation were the Midianites, who are the descendants of Keturah, the wife Abraham took in his old age after the death of Sarah. Moses' father-in-law, a priest of Midian, has supported them in time past and was always welcome in their midst. Not only because of his daughter Zipporah but because he shared their faith in YHWH. When he visited them at Mount Sinai, Jethro had renounced his gods for YHWH, surprising his daughter. Moses had been so happy with him that he had begged him to remain with them, perhaps to keep him from going back to the Midianites' worship of idols.

Since the death of Miriam, Mahlah looked more than ever for an opportunity to converse with Zipporah. She had not had another opportunity since the last time after the death of her father. So she prayed for another chance to meet with Zipporah. She had lots of questions she wanted to get true answers to, rather than people's speculations. She was curious about her sons Gershom and Eliezer. She wanted to know why they were not part of the leadership, as were the sons of Aaron, and even Miriam's son, Hur, who was not even a Levite. She also wanted to know the true picture of her relationship with her late sister-in-law. She and her mother had somewhat been glad to see her grandmother go, so she wandered if it was same with Zipporah. Not only had their grandmother been a sour person, but during her last few years she had become a permanent invalid. She was alone uprooting some vegetables for dinner from a vegetable garden they had discovered not too far from their tent. Noah was with their mother while the other three were taking care of their herd.

"Mahlah come quick," shouted Hoglah as she ran and stopped short a few feet from her sister. "The pregnant black and white ewe is dying." They both ran quickly to the plot of land where they kept their livestock. They were experiencing draught like they have never seen before. It had started shortly after Miriam's death, and they feared that it might be related to her absence. She outran Hoglah to the animal shed where they kept their herd. The ewe was lying on its side with its protruding pregnant belly sticking out and its hooves up. Mahlah rolled up her sleeves and tied her veil round her waist. "I need someone who can tear up the belly and rescue the calves." "I can do that," offered Tirzah. "You will not. We need a man who is adept at this." "Well neither uncle Baruch nor his sons can help now. Let me do this," Tirzah insisted. "No!" Hoglah and Mahlah shouted in unison. Their uncle Baruch took the vow of a Nazarite last year, a vow of separation unto the Lord. As a result he could not do too many things right now. He could not drink wine or fermented drinks. No razor could touch his head and there were certain situations he must not be involved in such as this. Even if his mother or father were to die, he was forbidden to go near. Thank God his parents were already dead. His sons were in the military camp, training seriously for an anticipated war as they prepared to leave Kadesh Barnea.

Mahlah put her hand over the animal's belly and could feel the movement of limbs that belonged to four or more lambs. Perhaps it was best that they did not make it, as they may not survive this draught. She was grateful they had not lost any of their limited animals to the draught. "There is something going on at the tent of meeting. The people are protesting about the lack of water," Noah, who had remained in the tent to mind their mother and other domestic things, came to inform her sisters. Mahlah was torn between leaving the ewe and going to the arena which was more important. Tirzah volunteered to stay with the animal till it passed.

When they got to the arena, they could hardly hear what was being said, as they were far at the back, straining their necks to see what was going on. She strained her neck to catch a glimpse of Moses. Moses was always calm in the midst of any catastrophe. She could see him from his chest up. He was wearing an ephod and breast piece lined with onyx, topaz, and sapphire, and his eyes matched the sapphire, contrasting with his wool-white hair. Even with the circumstance at hand, she could not help admiring this great man. The people started to calm down as Moses raised his staff, ordering the people to be silent. "How many times must we go through this?" he asked. "Have you forgotten so soon all that YHWH has done, taking care of us all these years in the wilderness? Do you think he will abandon you now, you stiff-necked people?" Moses and Aaron moved away from the people and went to the entrance to the tent of meeting. They fell face down and must have communicated their dilemma to YHWH. Soon enough they returned to the people, asking them to follow them to a big rock close by the camp. Moses raised his staff and struck the rock twice, and the next thing they saw was water pouring out of the rock. This was the first time Mahlah and her sisters were having a first-hand experience of a miracle apart from the manna that fell every morning like dew. This was different. The people exclaimed excitedly like little children. Some rushed forward to drink from the rock while some fell on their knees praising the Lord.

The events of the day had been too much for Mahlah. She had never had such a flood of different emotions in a day. By the time they got back to the dying ewe with some water, hoping they could salvage the situation, they met a surprise. Tirzah had single-handedly cut open the ewe's belly and was attending to five live lambs. They were speechless. Even though she was happy that

Tirzah had saved the lambs, she was nevertheless concerned. Her little sister was too tough for a young lady. They had joined her excitedly and finished up. Now they were in their tent and chatting excitedly about all that had happened. "Mother, we saw for ourselves today the hand of YHWH just like you have always told us." Noah faced her mother, including her in their conversation, something the others rarely did. "It was amazing mother." She continued looking into her face for a response but got none. Just as she was about to turn away from her, disappointed, Noah caught a glimpse of a smile from their mother and shouted out in surprise. They'd lived these past years for this moment. "Girls, come over here," she called out, and all her sisters gathered. In a voice so low and raspy, their mother said, "I am proud of you girls. I appreciate your patience with me and am happy that you are able to survive on your own. Your father was my life. He was a good husband and a good father. Even though he made a mistake breaking the law, to this family he was a hero and will remain a hero. I know he died for his own sins and my prayer is for you, my daughters, to be totally separated and dissociated from that, especially when you get to the promised land." Noah took a suspicious look at her mother and knew exactly what she was doing. She was giving her final speech. Noah stooped down and held her mother in her arms as quiet tears dropped to her face. Mahlah threw her arms round her mother and said, "Mother, we need you. We need you to be here for us. Please, we can all survive together." And because she could not hold back her tears, she ran out of the tent.

## 18

SHE COULD NOT BELIEVE her luck when she ran into the tall regal figure she had been praying to see for months. She held out her arms and took Mahlah in her arms while she continued to cry for a while. "Take your time, let it all out, it will help." Mahlah looked up at her, grateful for her comforting arms. It was twilight. The sun was setting in the horizon to the west of the camp. "Everyone is celebrating the miracle of the water from the rock, what has upset you child?" She waited patiently for Mahlah to gather herself. Because Mahlah was hurting because of her mother she began with asking Zipporah about her own mother. "The last time we spoke you never mentioned your mother. Do you not miss her as you do your father and sisters?" Mahlah asked, hoping to get all the answers she wanted tonight. This woman was an enigma to her and very few people knew about her in the camp. She was a very private person. "I lost my mother way before I met Moses and left Midian. Perhaps if she had been alive I would never have returned to my husband." Mahlah looked surprised. So it was true that Moses had sent her away at some point. "After the great deliverance from Egypt and we got to Mount Sinai, my husband and I just could not agree on anything anymore. He became a workaholic, more concerned about the people of Israel than he was about me and his sons. I told him to choose between me and the people and he chose the people. He sent me away with our sons to Midian. I was of course glad to be home, but my father would have none of it. My father and Moses have an unusual bond. It started from the time he came as an alien to work with my father in Midian. My father believed that when you are married to a man, there is no more room for you in his house. You belong to your husband. So he brought me and our sons back to him in Sinai, our rightful place you would say. My father remained with us for some time in Sinai as Moses would not let him return home. While my father was with us he saw for himself how my husband overworked himself. He was the one who advised to appoint the judges we have today. I was so thankful for that, hoping that my husband would spend more time with me, but it did not avail much. Well, I have since then given him up to YHWH. In between the time he spends in the tabernacle and the time he retreats into the mountains, I rarely see him. I know he loves the Lord and he is a holy man but how I wish for those days in Midian." Zipporah heaved a sigh. Mahlah kept quiet, hoping she would go on and she did. "When I met my husband, I had imagined a life of royalty in Egypt. I never imagined that I, the daughter of Jethro, would become a nomad wandering in the desert." "Your sons are Israelites aren't they?" "Of course they are, even though I resisted their circumcision. Not like it has not done them any good. They do not hold any position of importance in Israel like Aaron's sons. I was too much of a heathen for my sister in-law." "I'm sorry," Mahlah offered, not knowing what to say. "It is not your fault, but I will advise you to choose your husband carefully if you have the choice. I suppose your mother is dead, too." "No, she is not but she is as good as dead." "Really, why would you say such a thing?" Mahlah immediately regretted saying that. She did not want Zipporah to think her callous. "Since my father died over four years ago, we have not had our mother. Physically she is there but she is like an Egyptian mummy. She does not talk to us. She is not involved in anything we do. I know she'd rather go and be with her husband than remain with us. This evening she made that clear." "Oh that must be terrible for you and your sisters, I can imagine." "Can I ask you another personal question?" "Sure you can." Zipporah was encouraging her. "What is Moses like?" "Really, you mean apart from being the great mighty man of God," she said with laughter in her voice, and Mahlah was glad to see she had a good sense of humor. "Well I will tell you this. That man loves the Lord and his people. He is compassionate and protective of his people, especially the women and children. He saved me and my sisters in Midian from some unscrupulous shepherds who tried to take advantage of us because of our gender. He does not compromise the things of the Lord. As great as he appears, he knows his limitations and weaknesses. He is a very humble man. Many times he could have given up on these people but no, he will rather die on their behalf. His greatest weakness though is his bad temper. Can you imagine a man who suffered for forty days and forty nights fasting and getting the tablets of law from YHWH? He returned and then broke the very tablets that had kept him sleepless and hungry for forty days?" Mahlah listened with four ears, not believing her luck. Zipporah had just answered all her questions and more. "He is truly amazing. Thank you for sharing all this with me, I really appreciate you talking to me." "I told you the other time that your family reminds me of mine in Midian. That is why I am fond of you. I have never told anybody in the whole of this camp the things I have shared with you, you understand." Mahlah nodded respectfully. "Can I ask one more question? Do you think a family of women could approach your husband to demand their rights and not be punished?" "Well I do not know if that were possible but I do know that he is very considerate of all and he is just." "You know my sisters and I have always admired you. If we make it to the promised land, any possibility that you could attend my wedding ceremony?" "So you are getting married, who is the lucky man?" Mahlah cleared her throat. "Well there is none right now. I am just planning for the future." "Well then I will be seeing you around. Take care of yourself and your family," Zipporrah said, ending the conversation. Mahlah stood for a long time on the same spot where Zipporah left her. She was euphoric. She felt she had found a friend and a mentor in Zipporah.

# 19

"A NEW MONTH BEGINS TODAY!" Mahlah and her friend Tammuz who was visiting heard the messengers announced as they passed their tent, their bells ringing. The last month had been too long for her. The months were either twenty-nine or thirty days, depending on when the new moon is observed by two independent reliable eye witnesses. The witnesses after seeing the moon report to the assembly of leaders, who then send out messengers to announce the beginning of the month. The first day of the month was always exciting for the women because it was *Rosh Chodesh*, a minor festival when women do not work. However, there was no excitement for her, as this always left them one day behind their work schedule. Seeing the messengers reminded her of their current affair. Messengers were sent a week ago by Moses to the king of Edom to negotiate for passage through his land. They were confident that they would receive a favorable response because of the ties they had with the Edomites. There was high expectation and a lot of excitement in the air as Canaan appeared to be closer. The promised land was in view and she was strategizing just like every family was. When would be the right time to broach this subject of their father's inheritance with the leaders, she'd asked herself over and over. She had waited for her uncle Baruch to end his Nazirite's vow so she could discuss with him first. Thank God he was in the process of ending the vow. She suspected the scandal of his second wife, whom he ended up divorcing, and the loss of his dear brother, her father, had driven him to take those vows. He had been away from social life for two years. With his help, she and her sisters were going to fight for their rights. Thinking about her sisters, she was happy and was worried at the same time. They were doing well so far, for a family of only women.

## Their Father's Heirs

Noah, God bless her, has persisted with their mother, not giving up. As their mother grew weaker and weaker, she'd lost the control of her sphincters and Noah had become her full-time nurse. She never complained and never demanded that her sisters be more involved. She was a natural caregiver and could probably make a living nursing the sick, Mahlah predicted. She herself was trained in midwifery. Hoglah made perfumes. Milcah was the head shepherdess of their herd of livestock, though they all took turns in helping. Tirzah was very skilled in using weapons and doing things men do. They all had something going for them, even though Tirzah's was objectionable. Milcah like Hoglah was lost in a world of romance right now, something they all teased her mercilessly about. She was in love with another handsome Benjamite who showered her with lots of gifts. When she turned eighteen last summer he had given her the loveliest pair of earrings with a matching nose ring that they had all envied, except for Tirzah. They wanted to get married this year but Mahlah had convinced them to wait for another year. She had told Milcah that they needed to wait for Canaan, convinced it would be very soon. Tirzah was fifteen now but still did not behave like a lady. Her interests were a source of concern to Mahlah. Her new preoccupation was war. She had been spending a lot of time with Uncle Baruch's son Adiel, who suffered some war injuries and was now home to recuperate. Adiel was teaching her about all the intricacies of military training and war. He regaled her with tales daily of the battles they had faced and won. And now Tirzah has taken to training like a soldier, she wondered to what purpose. She woke up every day before the sun rose, and at the back of their tent they would hear her grunting as she aimed her spear and banged her makeshift shield. Her dresses were different from what was in vogue for every young lady. Her dress style gave her more allowance as the skirt was separated in the middle and wrapped around each leg. She tried to be firm with Tirzah but it was difficult because she was her sister and not her mother or father. Her mother would have been successful at this if she was herself but she was oblivious to everything now. Tirzah was getting out of hand and she could not afford to get any of her father's siblings involved because she trusted none except Uncle Baruch, who had been out of circulation for the last two years. Tirzah often traveled miles hiding to watch the soldiers train at the training grounds, a very risky adventure if caught. Her mother had always said that Tirzah was something their father created in his desperation for a son. "Well, Mother, I think you are right," she muttered under her breath.

Her friend Tammuz was getting married in a few days and all she talked about these days was marriage. "Are you listening to me, Mahlah? I said you should not allow Hoglah and Milcah to beat you to it." Tammuz, with one hand on her waist and the other hand gesticulating, was lecturing her as she walked her home. She was of the tribe of Ephraim and they have been friends since they were about eight. Tammuz was not only her closest friend but she made her laugh all the time, a medicine for her often troubled soul. "Did you hear about the mission to Edom? In no time we would be in Canaan, drinking milk and eating all the honey." Mahlah diverted their talk, causing her friend to hiss in exasperation. Since they turned twenty-eight, Tammuz has been on their case, laughing at herself and her friend. She had jokingly referred to herself and Mahlah as old maids that were going to end up delivering so many babies for other women as midwives, but never having their own. She had two close friends who were opposite in character, Tammuz and Eliana. While Eliana was very careful and sensible, Tammuz was bold and very outspoken. Her wedding that was about to take place had been practically engineered by her. The bridegroom was her father's friend who had lost his wife two years ago. She had gladly accepted to help him when her parents asked her to, all along scheming for a tie in matrimony. Tammuz said she had always liked him, even as a child, because he always gave her gifts. Moreover, she said, after she'd learned that her biological clock was ticking away, she had to do something real quick. The midwives believed that the older a woman became when she married the more difficult it was for her to have babies. They were both above the upper limit of the age believed to be best for reproduction. The midwives believed the best age was from sixteen to twenty-four. From observation, women younger than sixteen and above thirty did not do well with pregnancy and child birth. Mahlah, concerned that the man was too old, tried to talk her friend out of it, but Tammuz had insisted it was the best she could do since she was not as comely as Mahlah and her sisters. "Quit worrying about me and get yourself a husband so Milcah can marry her Prince Charming. Has Noah finished my wedding dress?" "Which is more important, your dress or my marriage?" Mahlah joked. "My dress of course," Tammuz responded, smiling lovingly at her friend. "And guess what I have for you? Palm dates, your favorite. Let's celebrate Rosh Chodesh."

## 20

Mahlah had attended several weddings in her lifetime, but Tammuz's wedding, which had taken place two days ago, had been different. She had been only a guest at most of the weddings she'd attended in the past. For the first time, she had fully participated and been the closest person to the bride outside the bride's immediate family. She had felt like a sister was taken away from her. Now she felt prepared for her sisters' weddings, having survived her best friend's own. In addition, she learned the details of a marriage ceremony firsthand. Tammuz had looked very beautiful and her groom did not appear too old looking after all. And she realized that her friend was not just materialistic with her choice of groom but actually shared some deep affection with her husband. She had caught the exchange of looks between them when Tammuz was asked to circle her husband during the ceremony. The food and wine had been surplus. The dance had been lively and fun with Tammuz dancing her heart out. She'd never seen her friend that happy. The only low point of the wedding for her had been when Tammuz received a Ketubah, a writing spelling out her husband's obligations to her and the conditions of inheritance in the case of his death. Considering the age gap between her friend and her bridegroom, that part had made everyone uncomfortable. She was sure that the reading of the Ketubah was sure to have created doubts in the hearts of many about Tammuz professed love. Outside a romantic involvement of two consenting lovers there were three ways men acquire wives in their community; through money, by contract, or sexual intercourse. A wealthy man could use his money to literally buy a wife. Two families could draw up an agreement to couple their son and daughter in marriage. And rarely a man might compromise a virgin's dignity, thereby forcing her to become his wife. Whatever way they acquired wives, they all paid a dowry. She could not quite place her friend's courtship in any of these categories, because from all indication she had initiated this relationship out of desperation. During the wedding, however, she was reassured that her friend's marriage would work since they appeared to have this mutual understanding. Her mother always said that marriage did not always have to be about falling madly in love but could work just as well based on mutual understanding. She herself was beginning to drop her childhood fantasies about falling in love. Her mother was not in love with her father when she married him but look at how they turned out. She concluded that she would take her friend's advice and be open to any good man who understood her enough to want her for his wife. But for now, she had a grave matter to deal with, their rights to their father's inheritance. She was going to speak with Uncle Baruch and then look for the earliest opportunity to go before the council of elders to present their case.

    At last Mahlah had her talk with her uncle Baruch and wished he had been more reassuring. He'd practically told her what she was considering was impossible. He said that in all his six decades of life he had not heard or seen it happen. It was not in their law, and even before the law it was not in their culture. He however advised that she start with the elders of their tribe and see what they would say. Mahlah was disappointed but not discouraged. She was determined to go ahead with her plans because it is what their father would have wanted. Their father had died by his own sin and was not listed among those that rebelled. He was not part of Korah and company who were sworn never to take part in the inheritance of the promised land. Her sisters were with her all the way, understanding the risk involved. She was going to take some time and fast before they proceeded. She grew up seeing her parents fast in difficult situations and winning.

    That same week the messengers that were sent to Edom returned after five days. A general assembly was summoned and she was standing deep in a large crowd of women behind the men of their tribe as they listened to Moses. Apparently the mission did not go as expected. The king of Edom was refusing to let them pass through his land. Furthermore, he was threatening them, breathing fire and brimstone. He threatened to attack them with his massive army if they attempted to come near. Moses was telling them that if they were to go to war with the Edomites he was sure of victory, but it was not YHWH's wish for them to fight them, because they were their brothers. So the plan was for them to turn back and go toward Mount Hor, a town at the edge of the territory of Edom. When the assembly disbanded, Mahlah sought out her uncle Baruch. "Uncle what does this mean? Are there going to be further delays?" "You heard the man of God, we are going ahead anyway. Mount Hor is an alternative route. The only concern is that this will likely bring us face to face with our enemies the Amorites. We were even willing to pay for our passage, but the Edomites refused. That is strange." Her uncle was able to discuss such matters with her just as he would with any other man without difficulty. He had watched her mature and take over her father's house like any son would have and was impressed. "What are the Edomites afraid of?" Mahlah asked her uncle. "Well I think it may just be the age-old rivalry that was between our father Jacob and their father Esau." "Really, I thought that was all in the past and had been resolved anyway?" "Ever heard that the sins of the fathers live after their children?" Mahlah frowned at that. "Speaking about the sins of the fathers, do you think my father's case could stand in the way of—you know what?" "Truly Mahlah, I do not know for certain. All I know is that if a man's way pleases the Lord, anything is possible. And remember YHWH is slow to anger and abounding in love." "Thank you, Uncle." Mahlah loved talking with her uncle, he was full of wisdom.

# 21

"Are you sure, Tirzah, that you heard correctly? The high priest was not known to be sick. Just the other day he and Moses ordained Eleazar." Mahlah was in disbelief, while Noah was weeping as loudly as she had done when they had lost their father. They were all in disbelief. Tirzah has just brought them news that the high priest Aaron was dead. He had given the most powerful teaching on the laws during the Sabbath two days ago and afterward he had left for the mountain with Moses on divine assignment, they'd all assumed. Now Tirzah was telling them that Moses had returned today and announced that their beloved high priest was dead. Mahlah was beginning to add one and one together. "Now I understand the ordination of Eleazar as the high priest just days before." She had initially thought that it was because Aaron was aged and had become too slow in discharging his priestly duties. Oh, poor Moses. Two years ago they had lost Miriam at Kadesh, now Aaron was gone. They were more than just leaders in the camp, they were his blood. Apart from his wife and sons they were his only family. It was sad. Mahlah feared that they were going to be grounded for some time and she was getting more and more anxious for Canaan.

At the assembly, Moses sorrowfully narrated to the people that YHWH had warned him of Aaron's death and commanded him to transfer the priesthood to Eleazar. He told them the pain he went through leading Aaron to die on the mountain top. He confessed that this was the repercussion for what happened at Kadesh. He admitted that he had been so enraged with the people and their bitter complaints that he had struck the rock twice with his staff instead of speaking to the rock as YHWH had commanded. He warned them that they should also prepare for his own death because YHWH had told him neither he nor Aaron would lead them into the promised land. The people responded with more wailing and distress when he said this. The whole camp mourned Aaron for thirty days, greatly saddened by the turn of events. They were worried about getting to the promised land without Moses or Aaron. Everything suddenly looked bleak and gloomy. Who could fill Moses shoes? Who could possibly take the place of Moses? Mahlah deliberated miserably.

Forty days after Aaron's death, they were still recovering from the shock when the trumpet was sounded to convene every soldier in the camp. "The king of Arad got information that we are moving in their direction toward Atharim and he is planning to attack us. This is not the first time he is doing this. The last time this happened we lost a lot of soldiers at Hormah, but this time Moses said YHWH is giving them to us if the people would not be intimidated." Tirzah was reiterating to her sisters what was going on. Mahlah wondered how she got this firsthand information when she was not a soldier. "Tirzah, how do you know this when there has not been enough time between the assembly and for us to hear from the soldiers?" "Never mind how I got the news, mind the news," she said with a superior air. Mahlah hated the fact that Tirzah might be keeping things from them or doing things she should not be doing. "In the midst of all that is going on, I want us all to focus on our primary concern. This is what will determine where we go from here. I spoke to Uncle Baruch and he said it was an impossible case. I have decided to give myself to prayer and fasting and you should join me." "You fight for your right, not pray about it," Tirzah said. "How do you fight for your right? You think it is physical? Don't you know that even Moses, before he does anything in the physical, he deals with it in the spiritual first?" Mahlah explained. Hoglah, looking in Tirzah's direction, joked, "She thinks she is the long-desired son of Zelophehad and a soldier at that." The four older sisters laughed while Tirzah pouted. "I do not think I am a man, I am just different. Everybody says that." "Well don't let that get into your head, you are just like any of us, a lady," Mahlah said with a note of finality. Determined to shift the attention from her, Tirzah changed the subject. "Well would you believe that we journeyed here forty years ago?" "How would you know? None of us were born then," Milcah asked, frowning. "Our leaders do not want us to know, but we have been going in circles trying to get to the promised land." "No we have not!" Milcah insisted. Mahlah kept quiet, knowing exactly what Tirzah was talking about, because Uncle Baruch had shared it with her. The older generation did not want to discourage their generation, so it was something they did not talk about. Exactly forty years ago they had been in this same geography with similar events as were happening now. Uncle Baruch said it was like a recurring dream, the drought and the water then from the rock. At this same site they had fought with the Amalekites and Canaanites. A fatal war with many Isrealites captured and killed in Hormah. Mahlah wondered if history will not repeat itself now. With the loss of Aaron and what Moses told them the other day, their soldiers were going to need some extra motivation. Their capability was not in doubt, for they were highly trained with captains like Joshua and Caleb, and of course with YHWH on their side. Their math in war was five Hebrew soldiers defeating one hundred enemy soldiers and one hundred of them taking ten thousand. It was why their enemies came in droves against them. Some of their soldiers had reported strange events like seeing strange mighty men fight on their sides in the middle of battles. That can only be YHWH's intervention. Mahlah concluded she would not worry too much with all these antecedents. The king of Arad would not even live to regret his actions.

## 22

WHILE THE WOMEN, CHILDREN, and men that were not at war because of age or infirmity went about a near normal daily routine, the war between the Israelites and the Canaanites of Arad waged on. Every now and then, they felt the ground trembled like there was an earthquake, they heard thundering voices of war cries from afar, but none were afraid. The high priest Eleazar and the Levites did not leave the tabernacle as they fought their own war spiritually. In the midst of all these, women were giving birth and male children were being circumcised but not named because their fathers were not there. This was the time when many would be named Ben-oni—son of sorrows, if their fathers did not make it back. And some would be named Achshiyarshu—great warrior, if otherwise. "If my husband does not survive the war and I have to name my baby, I want to name him Eitan." Her friend Tammuz who was expecting her baby in few weeks began a rhetoric on child naming. "I would hate for my son to be called Ben-oni." Mahlah scolded her for being more concerned about the name of an unborn child than her husband at war. Names were of utmost importance among her people. You either lived up to your name or you became the very opposite of your name. Some names told a story not necessarily about the bearer but about their parents' experiences, and God help you if the experience was bad. Mahlah reassured her friend and they both laughed over her own name and her sisters'. Their parents had named them, it seemed, based on what happened with each pregnancy. With her first pregnancy her mother had been very ill and swollen, and they had given her the name Mahlah, which meant "infirmity" or "fat." Thank God that she was nothing like that. Next was Noah, which meant "movement," because she had been very active in the womb, kicking so much and deceiving their father into thinking she was a boy. Also because during Noah's pregnancy, they had moved camp several times. Hoglah, meaning "dancing," was because their mother had been dancing when she broke her water, and Hoglah, true to her name, loved to dance. Because she had faced so much opposition from their grandmother and yet received much love and support from their father at the time of Milcah, they named her "Queen." Milcah, with her exotic looks, could truly pass for a queen. Tirzah's name meant "pleasing," and Mahlah did not know why. All she remembered was how disappointed her father had been and she was grateful they did not name her "Disappointment." Even Tammuz herself was not thrilled about her name. She joked that her parents could not be bothered, so they named her after the month of her birth Tammuz.

Mahlah was walking home later on from Tammuz's place and admiring the different tents she walked by. She marveled at the ingenuity of her people. The king of Egypt had taken undue advantage of this. Her people had been the major labor force in Egypt, mining and building the cities of Egypt. No people could match them in skills. They had people with unusual abilities and knowledge of all kinds of crafts. They had designers, embroiderers, weavers who were specially gifted to furnish the tabernacle. They had blacksmiths who furnished them with every form of weaponry. Not only did they have the skills but they were able to teach it to their children, passing it from one generation to the other. One of the sons of Ohaliab of the tribe of Dan recently created a metal dress for the upper torso and a metal cap for the soldiers. The soldiers were right now testing it at war. Mahlah could only imagine what glorious cities and structures they would create in the promised land. It would be the envy of the world! She had asked her uncle the other day to educate her on the territory of Canaan because she was confused like so many of her generation. It was confusing because it was not just one state like Egypt, but a group of different nations within a territory. She learned that the Canaanite group consisted of the Amorites, the Moabites, the Jebusites, the Edomites, and the Syrians. The land extended from the brook of Egypt to the Jordan River valley. It was a lot of land

and they should be able to get their father's portion. Her uncle said that YHWH designed for them to take over this land because the Canaanites were cursed. They worshipped Baal and his wife Ashteroth through temple prostitution, human sacrifice, and orgies. She had heard gruesome stories of parents burning their children alive as sacrifices to these gods.

"Mahlah, come quickly, it is Mother!" Hoglah ran up to her as she approached their tent. She hated the sound of this call, as it reminded her of the time her father had died. She had been anticipating this for some time so she was not taken aback. Their mother had grown weaker by the hour in recent days. She had stopped eating or drinking completely. She was always lying so still with her eyes shut as if dead. She calmly walked pass their tent and went to look for Milcah who was with the animals. Getting there, she looked through their makeshift sheep pens and found her bent over a ram. She took a deep breath and told her plainly in an emotionless voice, "I believe mother is dead." Milcah dropped the hay in her hand and without wasting one moment began to run to their tent. Mahlah caught up with her as cool as a cucumber. When they got to their mother, Noah had her in her arms, holding so tight as if to squeeze her back to life. They all tore their dresses in mourning as the custom demanded. Mahlah, still calm and collected, noticed that Tirzah was missing. She had forbidden her to go anywhere near the area of battle when she had seen her that morning with a complete set of armor. None of them knew where she had gotten the armor from and none knew where she was. Planning to go back out and announce her mother's death to their relatives, and at the same time to find Tirzah, Mahlah told her sisters the obvious. "We need to prepare her for burial immediately. This is a most inappropriate time but we will have to manage." They had a few male relatives around but they were old, all the young, able men were at war. She would get one of the old male relatives to preside over the burial and she and her sisters would handle the rest. It shouldn't be too hard for them, as their mother over the years had become so shrunken like a melon abandoned in the sun. She imagined she was happy now, free from the life that no longer held any appeal for her. She had rejected them for their father. She knew they were not only going to miss their mother but they would never know the joy of having her around to help them nurse her grandchildren. Tammuz would never have to lift a finger after having a baby because her mother would be there to do everything for her. It was a tradition their women relished after nine to ten months of carrying and supporting another life all by themselves.

## 23

THEY MANAGED BETWEEN THEMSELVES and two old uncles to put their mother to rest. Now Mahlah and her sisters were observing Shiva, the seven days of mourning and doing nothing. Still there was no Tirzah in sight and she refused to raise an alarm, lest that get her into trouble. It would be serious trouble indeed, Mahlah had a strong feeling, that her sister was on the battle ground. She could only pray that she was just observing and not foolish enough to actually participate. She had shared her suspicion with the others and warned them to keep it secret between them. They were complying so far, as they kept telling their visitors who inquired of Tirzah that she wanted to be alone somewhere in the tent. "Oh she must be devastated," commented one of their neighbors. "If only you knew where she really was, you would be devastated," Mahlah thought sarcastically. There was no dirge playing this time around because the time was inappropriate for any ceremony. They had been lucky to get the go ahead from the elders to bury their mother as they did. She had not expected any more than this.

On the evening of the fifth day of mourning, Tirzah appeared. They were together in their tent praying for their mother and for the remaining days to pass quickly enough so they could get on with their lives. She tiptoed into the tent thinking they were asleep. "Bat Zelophehad, where have you been for the past one week? No descent young lady goes off like that. I am so upset with you and am taking this to Uncle Baruch," Mahlah burst out in one breath while her sisters looked at Tirzah as if she were unreal. "Please not Uncle Baruch, I beg you. I will confess everything I promise. I heard that mother passed on, please allow me mourn my mother first." And she began to cry. Mahlah could not believe her response, but Noah rose up and took her in her arms, unable to resist her baby sister, just like their mother couldn't when she lived.

"I don't care for that Tirzah. If you cared so much about mother you would not have done what you did," Mahlah insisted, refusing to let her off so easily. "Please let her be, for Mother's sake. You don't want the neighbors to hear this do you?" Noah defended her sister. "I will let it lie low for now, but it's going nowhere. As soon as Shiva is over, you have a lot of explaining to do, young lady," Mahlah finally backed down.

A few days later the war was over and they won. There was a lot of jubilation in the camp. Fathers, sons, uncles, and brothers were returning to their family after a long battle with the Canaanites in Arad. The whole month had been ridden with a lot of anxiety. It was wonderful to know that they were free now. "I could have told you about this outcome before the soldiers returned, but the circumstances did not permit me." "Really, you mean you knew the outcome of this war as of the time you returned?" asked Milcah in amazement. "Well, I guess I may as well tell you everything now. I convinced Ben-Ohaliab to make me a helmet so I could hide my hair. I had a complete armor thanks to the souvenirs that Dor's parents gave me last year." Tirzah paused, then said dramatically, "Prepare to be shocked sisters, I fought in that war!" They were together sharing a meal of lamb stew with manna. "Keep your voice down, Tirzah. No one should overhear this," a concerned Noah quickly interjected, fearful that someone might have heard. "Calm down, Noah, no one is going to find out. Tirzah, is there any other person apart from us that knows this?" asked Mahlah. Tirzah looked down ashamed and for a moment feared the possibility of being found out. "Cousin Adiel and Eitan know." "I suspected Adiel knew, but how does Eitan know?" Mahlah asked, looking puzzled. Adiel was the one who got Tirzah started in the first place with all the stories of war he shared with her. But Eitan had not been around, he found her out at the war. "I attached myself to his battalion. He noticed something strange about me from the onset and kept an eye on me. He noticed that I would not speak around the men and after a fight, I usually went into hiding, away from the others. He followed me on one occasion and found out I was no more than his own little female cousin. He was shocked and angry, but I begged him not to give me up. After reprimanding me, he admitted that I was impressive in battle, so much so that none of the men had noticed anything strange except for him." But she did not tell them about falling in love with Eitan. She still did not understand what had happened. It had happened so fast, one moment they had been exchanging heated words and the next moment she was in his arms. Eitan had been upset about it all and had made sure she left Arad immediately. He had personally escorted her halfway to the camp. She would never be able to face Eitan again. After all that happened, she was changing her mind fast about life. There was nothing pleasant about killing or watching another die. She was done with trying to be as strong as a man. Now she was ready for her sisters to make a lady out of her. Mahlah was in disbelief and afraid of her sister's crazy endeavor going public. She would be punished severely for deceiving the army. No woman had ever gone to war. "I will have to speak to him myself," Mahlah said. "Please no! He would never expose me. He made a vow." "If so, what problem do you have with me confirming that?" Mahlah saw the look of guilt and something else on her sister's face. Tirzah was blushing beet red, even with minimal light from the lamp. It was not difficult to see through her translucent skin. "Hmmm, I guess I will take your word that we are safe." "Yes, I promise you, and I will never ever do anything like this again. I want to be a lady now." Hoglah seized the opportunity to make sure Tirzah meant business. "Can we begin with that ridiculous dress you wear?" "Yes, and no more spears, shields, bows, and catapults. We need to hide them or throw them away," chipped in Noah, who hated these things because it unnerved her every time she saw Tirzah with them. "I am glad the war is over. My plan is for us to proceed with our request as soon as the thirty days of mourning mother are over. I am hoping that with all that has happened to us, we will get some sympathy from the elders and the judges. I want us to approach the assembly of elders first." Noah, always very cautious, asked, "Mahlah, are you sure that we can do this?" "Yes we can. We have to try for father's sake, and it is our right." Moses had elected elders from all the tribes to act as judges for any legal disputes, and they served as the first point of call. However, with difficult cases they refered the plaintiff to the high priest, who was an authority in interpreting the laws for the people. Still, if there was no resolution, the case would finally end on Moses' table. Even though this was the protocol, it was not a law to follow this pattern. Many a time people would go straight to Moses because of the nature or urgency of the case.

## 24

THEY WERE AT A valley in Moab and the daughters of Zelophehad, like every other Israelite, were trying to recover from a very strenuous and eventful journey. In the last one year, they had been through and to so many places in the desert. They had left Mount Hor and travelled a very long route along the Red Sea just to skirt around the Edomites, since they had denied them passage through their land. They had camped at Oboth, then at Iye Abarim, a very hot place in the desert facing the land of Moab. From there they had camped in the Zered valley and then at Arnon, a place between Moab and the territory of the Amorites. It had been a long journey with lack of water because it was that part of the desert where there was very minimal evidence of life. The places had been so arid that everyone had feared death from thirst and dehydration. It was no wonder Moses had pleaded with the king of Edom and even offered to pay for their passage through Edom. For the second time in her life, Mahlah witnessed firsthand another act of rebellion and defiance from the people. The people, flushed with the victory of the war against the Canaanites in Arad and perhaps a little overconfident, had become very impatient with the turn of events. They had questioned Moses' decision about not going to war with the Edomites. They had wanted to go back and fight the Edomites and forcefully go through their land, but Moses would not hear of it. A group had gone further, saying they regretted their escape from Egypt and that they detested everything about the journey, including their miraculous manna. She and her sisters were no saints, as they had also complained about the long, strenuous, and dry journey, but they never joined in the public protest. It had been a fearful event. She'd feared that finally they had broken the camel's back and only doom could follow. But just as her mother always recited to her, "YHWH was slow to anger and quick to forgive." They had been punished and then forgiven. The Lord sent venomous snakes into their camp and many people had died from snake bites. She was grateful that none of the people close to her, especially her sisters, had died. Milcah and two of Uncle Baruch's sons had been bitten by the snakes, but just at the right time, when YHWH forgave them and provided healing. Moses was instructed to make a bronze snake erected on a pole, and all anyone bitten had to do was look up at the bronze snake to be healed. Her cousin Adiel had nearly not made it. He had been so affected by the venom from the snake bite that he had not been able to keep his face up. It took his father and one of his brothers to practically hold his face up in the direction of the bronze snake. What a people they were. They had so quickly forgotten what had happened at the waters of Meribah after Miriam's death. She respected their leader Moses more than ever. He had been the one again who pleaded on their behalf, despite their insults and disrespect. With the way she saw him handle the whole situation, she had no doubt that when the time came for her sisters and her to make their appeal, they would find favor. She'd learned many lessons from the whole event. After the rebellion, Moses had led them to a well in Beer where they had found water. She'd learned that the Lord was just like a father. If she were to write a song about this, it would go thus: "Like a father he scolds and punishes for wrongdoing; that we might learn. Yet as a father he forgives every wrongdoing; so we know that he loves us. Still as a father he makes provision for all our needs; so we know that he always cares."

From Beer they had gone through Mattanah, Nahaliel, Bamoth, and now they were in a valley in Moab whose top overlooked a vast wasteland that they would have to traverse. Their cousins had come over, as they always did, to assist them in putting up their tent. These days they had many skillful young men in their midst who specialized in tent making, if you could afford to pay. But having their cousins help them was a blessing. They were all just waiting to exhale in the promised land. She was tired of putting up their tents only to pull them down again. For families who could afford the tent makers, she guessed it was no trouble.

The tent makers were very good though. In the past, their father had hired tent makers and then they gave them better tents than the ones they built themselves. Their skills added to making their dwellings beautiful. "How beautiful are your tents, Oh Jacob, your dwelling places, Oh Israel..." Foreigners had commended their camps. Their tents were built in different shapes and sizes, depending on the number of occupants and their taste. Their cousins were building a small one for them but it was nevertheless serious work. They constructed a framework first with the weather in mind. They elevated the framework and then crossed over the sides of the tent because they were in a place that was known for storms. If it were winter they would have dug into the grounds and sunk in the tents halfway. Next they created an inlet on top to serve as a ventilator and stove pipe for the cooking area. When they finished they stayed for supper, chatting and laughing, making Mahlah and her sisters very happy. There was no denying that they missed the presence of a male in their family. Since the incidence with Eitan on the battle grounds at Arad, Tirzah had made sure she was never within two feet of him until now. She was quiet while her four older sisters chatted comfortably with Eitan and his other brothers. But several times she caught him looking in her direction with questions in his eyes.

Two weeks into their settling in the valley of Moab, they were all still recovering from the strain of the journey. Mahlah, focused on their mission to make an appeal for their father's inheritance, was scheming conclusively with her sisters when Uncle Baruch walked in. "How are you daughters doing? I see that your cousins did a good job here." Since the death of their father, their uncle made sure they were never far from him when they set up camp. Having no daughters himself, his nieces became like his daughters. They respected him more than any of their father's siblings and over the years had grown closer to him and his sons. "Uncle, my feet are still swollen from the entire journey these past months," complained Hoglah. "No, your feet are only growing in proportion to your body," contradicted Tirzah, who loved to tease her big sister, whose size bordered on the side of voluptuousness more than fat. "Tirzah, I am not fat, I am just well endowed," Hoglah defended herself. "Please, not in the presence of Uncle Baruch, you two," Mahlah interjected. "Thank you, Mahlah, but I dare say that I am enjoying this. But more seriously, I have some uncomfortable news about the camp." "Is it about the rumor of another war?" Tirzah asked. "No, it is not a rumor. We requested for a passage through the territory of the Amorites but their king Sihon said no and is now declaring war against us." "But Uncle, we just got here," Milcah stated wearily. "From every indication, we are not far from concluding this journey. And the earlier we deal with all our enemies the better," their uncle answered. "So we are going to war with the Amorites," stated Milcah, again wearily. "I will take my leave now." Mahlah got up just as he was saying that. "Uncle, please, may I walk with you." She wanted to update him on what she had decided with her sisters about their novel request. "Uncle, I feel it is time to make our first appeal through the assembly. We have spent some time fasting and praying and I believe that we will be favored." "I have been praying for you, too, but you may have to still wait some more with the war and all." "But Uncle, how long do you think we will have to wait. It looks to me like we are going to be at war from now until we settle in the promised land." "I hate to admit that you may be right daughter. So do whatever you have in your mind, may God help you all." Mahlah took her uncle's right hand and gave him a kiss and curtsied, a sign of love and affection for a father. "What is going on between Eitan and Tirzah?" "Uncle, I have no idea, but I intend to find out." "Please do so and let me know." This was a common thing with Mahlah and her uncle. As the heads of their family, they made it their duty to know what was going on, and they often discussed together afterwards.

## 25

THE NOISE OF CELEBRATION in the camp was deafening, but exciting anyhow. They had prepared for one war with King Sihon, but they had ended up fighting two wars. The moment they defeated King Sihon of the Amorites and his entire army in the desert of Jahaz, King Og of Bashan had come against them with his vast army. YHWH gave them a double win, and easily, too, for they did not suffer many casualties. Not only did they put the two kings and their armies to the sword but they had acquired land that was now theirs. The land spanning the whole Transjordan, extending from the Arnon River at the midpoint of the Dead Sea to the Jabbok River, which empties into the Jordan River. They were delirious with joy at this accomplishment. There was an assembly and all they were doing was praising the Lord with songs and dance. Sacrifices of bulls, rams, and goats were given and there was much to eat and drink.

Mahlah was catching up with her friend Tammuz, who had a toddler and was pregnant again. Tammuz had not changed much with marriage except for gaining some weight. She was still as exuberant and funny as ever. As they ate and drank, she filled Mahlah up with rumors and some real events. "So how are you feeling, Tammuz, this second time around. I learned in midwifery that every pregnancy is different, do you feel it?" "I don't know about that, but I am just glad that I do not have to observe Niddah for at least the next one year. I hate Niddah!" Mahlah laughed at her friend but wondered about it, remembering that it was the one thing her mother complained about in life. Niddah was the period during menstruation when wives are separated from their husbands. At the end of it they undergo a ritual immersion to be made clean again. Their gist took a serious turn when she told her that Milcah's Benjamite was about to settle down with another woman that his parents arranged for." "What? How come Milcah doesn't know? She was with him three days ago celebrating his safe return from the war." "I guess he does not want her to know yet," answered Tammuz blithely. "Maybe he is not going along with his parents," countered Mahlah hopefully. She felt guilty because she had been the one who convinced Milcah to wait and had Uncle Baruch talk to the Benjamite. But whatever the case, she had not expected him to treat her sister disrespectfully. Milcah should be the first one to know and certainly if Tammuz knew then it must be the talk of the camp. "And he never told Milcah his parents did not approve of her," she wondered out loud. Immediately she left Tammuz, and Mahlah went to look for her sister Milcah. She found her with Hoglah, Noah, and a cousin, and it looked like she had gotten the news already. She was just gazing into the distance, smiling but not really involved in the ongoing discussion. It confirmed Tammuz story. It just made Mahlah more resolved to deal with the matter of their inheritance soon. The several acrid comments made by some people in their camp about their marital status were not lost on her. She'd heard an uncle say recently that if Mahlah and Noah waited any longer they would never find a man to marry them. She knew it would not be a difficult thing for them to find husbands because they were admired by many eligible men, with some having proposed already. But how could they just erase the existence of their father like that, because that is exactly what would happen. With no brother to inherit their father's portion of the land they were possessing, his name would never be mentioned again even though he was a firstborn.

    Weeks after the wars, they were once again settled in the land of the Amorites waiting for the next move toward the main land across the Jordan. The lands of Jezer and Hesbon where they were currently camping, were very rich, very good for livestock. It was a savanna where foliage and fauna were prolific, with several surrounding rivers. There was peace here, but for Mahlah there was no peace until they were able to meet with the council of elders. Tirzah had suggested that they go straight to the overall leader Moses, but she rejected the suggestion. With this approach of going through the elders and the high priest first, meeting with Moses would be made easier. They were ready now. Through Uncle Baruch they had made their request, and a meeting had been scheduled for the sixth hour tomorrow. She was more anxious about standing before the elders than standing before Moses. She at least had some information about Moses' character and personality, but the elders that made up the lower court she knew nothing of. Even Gamaliel, who was the head of their tribe, she barely knew. All she knew was what she remembered her father say in moments of anger. Her father had believed that Gamaliel never liked him like he did the other men of their tribe. This was a source of concern for her. What if he displayed that same antagonism toward them? Well, she would just have to believe the Lord would grant them favor, irrespective of who these men were.

It had been a long day for Mahlah and her sisters. They were returning from the meeting with the elders, which had not gone down well. They were disappointed but not defeated. "Did you see the looks on their faces when Mahlah stated our case." Tirzah was huffing and puffing in a rage. "I was so terrified. I almost wetted myself from fear," Noah said, looking actually terrified. "Well snap out of that terror because we are going to Moses," Mahlah, who was already thinking ahead on how to insist on their request, retorted. The elders had been shocked. Some of them had been nasty, reminding them that their father was not only dead but had died shamefully, leaving no son. They practically told them that on these grounds they had no rights, but Mahlah had responded boldly, "Yes, my father died for his own sins, but he was not a partaker of the rebellion of Korah. He was the firstborn of his father and a good man. Why should his name disappear from his clan because he had no son?" They had kept silent after this and then given their verdict almost immediately. Just as her uncle had told her beforehand, they said that it was not in their law and had never happened before that a woman should inherit her father's property. "I bet those uncles of ours would be glad now since they no doubt want it all for themselves," Tirzah blurted, still very angry. "Well they won't get it without a fight from us. Do you remember the men who could not participate in the Passover some years ago because they had been around the corpse of a loved one? Remember they went to Moses pleading their case and Moses took the case to YHWH and that law was reversed," Mahlah stated, hoping to encourage her sisters. "Do you think that would be our case? Or should we reconsider this case? I don't know that I can stand before Moses," Noah stated worriedly. "You mean we should allow father's name to disappear from his clan? You fight for your rights, Noah, not stand down. We will fight for father's name," responded Tirzah boldly. "Yes, we will soldier," Mahlah said, agreeing with her baby sister and at the same time teasing her. "We will all stay inside and pray until we get a word for our appearance at the tent of meeting." After the elders gave their verdict, Mahlah had requested to take their case to Moses, and they had agreed, telling them they would beckon them when the time was right. She hoped that it would not take forever. They needed to know their plight right away so they could get on with the part of their life they had put on a hold.

## 26

IN THE DAYS FOLLOWING their appearance before the assembly of elders, they limited their activities to the very basic duties, just as Mahlah had recommended. She said that they did not need the camp talking more than necessary at the sight of them. Of course the news would have gone round of their bold act and strange request. Some of their people, especially of their tribe, would berate them, some would sympathize with them. But whatever the case, Mahlah abhorred any form of talk. Yesterday their aunt Chava and her daughters had come to visit them, and for once their aunt was impressed with them. She told them if it worked out and the law was reversed she hoped to benefit. Tirzah had wittingly reminded her that she had brothers and now bore another man's name.

Milcah had somewhat recovered from her disappointment with her Benjamite with all they had going on. She'd told her sisters everything not shedding a tear. She'd accepted he was not her *"Bashert"* after all. She was glad they had not done the *Kiddushin*—the official acceptance of money or contract or sexual relationship offered by a prospective husband which binds a woman even though the marital relationship does not take effect until the *Nisuin*. Nisuin is done about a year after Kiddushin and completes the marriage process with a husband taking his wife to his home. Milcah had made attempts to return every gift that he had given to her, but her generous Benjamite would not take them back. Mahlah suggested that she sell the gifts or just keep them, but should never wear them again. She was glad that not too many people knew of her alliance with the Benjamite, as they had been very discreet, almost a clandestine affair. Ideally for a young lady and a man to be seen freely together they must have done Kiddushin officially by their custom. But surprisingly, Milcah's preferred choice for a husband still remained a Benjamite. Something Mahlah believed was unnecessarily overrated. The Benjamites were known as excellent marksmen and a lot of them were left-handed. They could sling stones at a hair's breadth and not miss. To be objective, the Benjamites were very good looking. They were tall and athletic, most maidens' dream.

"Milcah, you are daydreaming or thinking about your Benjamite." "Oh Hoglah, you read me too well. I was indeed thinking about him." "What about him? He does not deserve you, you are a queen, remember, that is your name." "Hoglah, I am worried. What if we do not get men that desire us enough to marry us. There are one, two, three, four, five of us. Our parents are no more and here we are undertaking something that has never happened in Israel." Hoglah faced her sister squarely, holding her hand. "Look at me and listen. We have a lot more going for us than a lot of young women. We are beautiful and talented, if I may say so, and if any man cannot see these qualities, the loss is theirs." Milcah, hearing her sister's reassuring words, held back her tears and smiled. They walked hand in hand into their tent to hear Mahlah hush Tirzah as they parted the curtains to enter. Hoglah, who could never handle being kept out of anything, immediately attacked her sisters. "We do not keep secrets in this family, so spill it, Tirzah." Tirzah looked at Noah and Mahlah helplessly. Noah rose from her seat and took Milcah in her arms as if to protect her. "What is it? Milcah can handle it," Hoglah insisted, hating the suspense. Mahlah cleared her throat and began talking. "Well our people are at it again. Some men have been frolicking with Moabite women and the news has gotten to Moses." "So what has that got to do with Milcah or us?" Hoglah asked puzzled. "They have committed a great evil in the sight of YHWH," Mahlah continued. "How so, I thought you said they were just frolicking with them?" Hoglah continued asking trying to follow her sister's direction of reasoning. "They did not stop at just having sexual affairs with these women but they joined in worshipping and making sacrifices to their gods. They took part in the fertility rites of Baal," Tirzah finished for Mahlah. "Idolatry!" Milcah exclaimed. It was the worst sin to commit. The first law commanded against idolatry and the second commandment was also against idolatry. At Mount Sinai idolatry had caused them the death of three thousand people in one day. Moses had gone up to the mountain to receive the law that was to govern them when they became a nation again after leaving Egypt. Moses had been gone for forty days and nights and by the time he returned the people had turned to another god. They had pressured Aaron into building for them a golden calf similar to the Egyptian bull-god Apis. At that time the law had not even been presented yet, and yet the repercussions had been grave. Now that they had had the law for forty years, read over and over to them, Mahlah could not imagine what will happen this time. She prayed this would not take them back in their journey now that they were so close to the promised land. "Still, what has this got to do with me personally that you did not want me to know?" Milcah faced Mahlah, fearing there was more. "Your Benjamite is one of those men," Tirzah again finished the gist. Milcah crumpled from her sister's arms to the floor. Then her sisters knew that she was not over her Benjamite and was not likely to ever forget him. Tirzah, wanting to lighten the whole situation and console her sister, said, "I think you should thank the Lord that he broke up with you. You would have become a widow even before becoming a wife." "Tirzah!" all four sisters shouted. Milcah began to cry all the tears she had held back since her breakup. Noah picked her up from the floor, guided her to her sleeping pallet, all the while whispering words of comfort to her. Mahlah sighed, fearing they were in for a long night and fearing this was going to be a distraction for their pending case. At least the people had something new to gossip about other Zelophehad's daughters' strange request. By tomorrow they would know all the details, as a hearing had been called for at the tent of meeting by Moses.

# 27

JUST AS EXPECTED, EVERY family was gathered at the tent of meeting. "Who are the men responsible for these wicked acts? How could you exchange the sweet vines of Israel for the poisonous apples of Moab? The ox knows his master, the donkey his owner's manger, but Israel does not know its owner. This is a disgrace. This is an insult to the God who brought you up and out of Egypt. How long will you continue to hold him in contempt?" A silence so thick that a sword could cut through followed Moses' address. "Now the Lord commands you to expose all the heads of the families involved in this this abomination in broad daylight. Each of you judges must put to death those of your men who joined in worshipping the Baal of Peor. This is the only way that the Lord's fierce anger will turn away from Israel." The women gasped loudly, the men were shocked into immobility. A loud wailing broke out as the people lifted their voices weeping and pleading. Mahlah just stood there with her sisters, dazed. She had tears streaming down her face and she wondered for the umpteenth time about this prevalent and recurring act of rebellion from her people. When will it stop, she asked over and over. Will they ever cease from inciting the wrath of YHWH? How many times will he forgive and overlook such acts? Why were the judges not moving? They had been instructed to kill those guilty, but they all just stood there. Almost immediately, a plague broke out in their midst, and people began collapsing left, right, and center. Moses had told them to stop wailing and obey in order to turn away YHWH's anger or else suffer a deadly plague. Just as he said this, people began to experience a flesh-eating disease that was so malignant that within half an hour the whole body was consumed. The camp was in chaos, with women wailing and screaming. With tears clouding her vision, Mahlah nearly missed an unbelievably foolhardy act of a young man whose name and tribe she did not know but prayed seriously that he did not belong to their tribe. While everyone was weeping, this young man walked through the crowd toward a tent, arm in arm with a foreign woman indecently dressed, right in front of Moses and the whole assembly. Before Moses could say anything else they saw Phinehas, the son of Eleazar, take a spear and follow the couple into the tent. Phinehas came back out with a bloodied spear and almost immediately the plague ceased. Apparently he'd driven the spear through the young man and into the woman's body, killing them both. The plague stopped completely, but not before thousands of people had died instantly from the plague. Amidst the horror of so many deaths in a few hours, there was a restrained cheer for Phinehas' heroic act. It was a bold act that was buying them another chance. Mahlah had never been this terrified in her entire life. She'd feared that they were all going to die as she watched men and women fall to the ground all around her. It turned out that the young man's name was Zimri, the son of Salu, the leader of a Simeonite family, and his lover was the daughter of a tribal chief of a Midianite family.

Hours later there was still much wailing in the camp as the dead bodies were removed for burial. There were corpses everywhere. The number of those who died exceeded even those who died in the Rebellion of Korah and his allies, twenty-four thousand gone, just like that. Mahlah was in a panic as she began to search all around, not only for her sisters, but also for her uncle Baruch and his house. When she found them all intact she fell on her knees to worship and thank the Lord for sparing her family again. Like every other tribe, their tribe had suffered loss, too, and many cousins and uncles were gone. The worst hit, it appeared, were the Simeonites, while the tribe of Levi had been totally spared. It took a day and a half to clear the camp of the dead bodies. After the mass burial they were gathered again at the tent of meeting for purification rites, and a sin offering was made for the whole assembly. Phinehas was celebrated as a hero and a word came for him. YHWH was making a covenant of peace with Phinehas for his zeal for YHWH's honor. Phinehas and his descendants would always have the honor of the priesthood forever. She could not help but wonder if the judges were not green with envy now. Phinehas was being honored because he had done what they had failed to do. YHWH also instructed that the Midianites were to be treated as enemies for life. When Moses said this, the whole assembly went really quiet while some people dared to look in the direction of Moses' wife Zipporah. This was going to be a very difficult situation. Mahlah felt sorry for Zipporah, and even Moses. The Midianites were her people and Moses had enjoyed a wonderful relationship with Jethro, his father-in-law. She knew Zipporrah would be heartbroken and would probably fight this, but they all knew once YHWH has spoken it was law. The Midianites have not helped matters themselves. For not too long ago, their elders had collaborated with Balak, the king of Moab, against the Israelites. They had hired a popular diviner named Balaam to curse Israel. They had failed, but the Israelites had been disappointed with the Midianites ever since. The absence of the leadership of Jethro, who was dead, was undeniably obvious. He had truly been a friend of Israel and not only just Moses' in-law.

After the unprecedented loss of lives, the whole camp tried settling again and moving on with life. For a lot of families this was not going to be an easy task. In as much as almost every family had been affected, there was still the usual business of gossiping and castigations. People wanted to know all who had been involved and what family or tribe was worst hit. So everywhere people were talking. She only wanted to erase that event from her memory and not talk about it. Milcah's Benjamite was one of the men that had been involved in the indecent act, and he and his whole family were gone. "Perhaps if he had not broken off with you, he would still be alive," Tirzah began in her "I know it all" voice. "No matter the circumstance of death, Tirzah, you must not speak disrespectfully of the dead," lectured Noah. "Moreover, that is presumptuous. What about the people who had not been directly involved and yet died?" Hoglah added. "Well, I am sure his family must have been aware of his affair with that Midianite woman," Tirzah continued. Mahlah looked at Milcah, who remained quiet and pensive, and decided to rescue her from Tirzah's inconsiderate and acrid comments. "We will not join the rumor mongers and backbiters in this camp. That is enough Tirzah."

## 28

MAHLAH DID NOT UNDERSTAND why she felt the way she did, but she did. There was an ongoing census. All those twenty years old or more who were men were being numbered from every family except hers. She imagined her father must have felt like this or worse. She felt like her family was ostracized. She felt like they did not belong. Even though she understood it was nobody's fault. YHWH had instructed Moses and Eleazar to carry out a census and number this group of people for the army. She had watched as the censoring Levite had passed their tent to Uncle Baruch's and had watched her cousins proudly displaying their qualifications—their gender. She was not jealous of her cousins but just wished her father's house could be numbered, too. If they had a brother, the story would have been different. It made her sad, but it made her also more determined to fight for their father's name. Mahlah's mind was in overdrive as she thought of possible ways to quickly realize this.

Because of the census, there was no working. The sisters were in their tent relaxing but bored. Tirzah, in her mischievous manner, began a topic she knew Mahlah would probably rather not talk about. "So because we do not have hair all over our face and body we do not qualify to be numbered?" Hoglah, Noah, and Milcah laughed at her spunk, but Mahlah refused to be amused. They had all watched together the censoring activity that was going on around them from the front of their tent. "It is not a laughing matter, Tirzah, they are only executing an order from above," Mahlah admonished. "I should have mentioned to them that I have fought in the army and therefore am more qualified than some of those young men," Tirzah continued. "Mahlah can I ask why you are upset?" Mahlah, wanting her sister to understand her feelings, explained, "Can't you see, Tirzah? It is like we do not have any value. I am feeling for father because it must have hurt him more. For something that was not in his control. I believe YHWH loves us all equally, whether male or female, and it is time for some things to change." "Yes, I agree with you. Things ought to change around here," Tirzah shouted excitedly. "Are you two trying to start a rebellion? 'Cause if you are, I will not be part of it," Noah said. Mahlah laughed, this time around seeing the look of terror on Noah's face. "I don't know about Tirzah, but what I am talking about is making our petition for our rights to father's inheritance." "Keep your voice down, I hear a footstep," Hoglah cut them short. They stopped talking and watched a tall figure stoop to enter their tent after calling out to warn them. It was their cousin Eitan. "Welcome," they all chorused excitedly, except Tirzah, who looked down. "To what do we owe this visit?" Milcah teased their very handsome cousin. "How is father holding up with all these talk of war? Are you men prepared for another battle?" Hoglah asked with concern. "Which do I answer first?" he chuckled. They were all used to such banter without any reservations because they were close. "I invited myself to an evening meal with my beautiful cousins." He said this looking at Tirzah, who refused to look at him. "I promised Uncle Baruch that I would come over about now to spend time with him," Tirzah quickly announced, standing to her feet, but Noah would not let her go. "Eitan is here to spend the evening with us, you should respect that. And I am sure Uncle knows that he is here." "In that case, let me help you with the meal then." "What! That is a miracle!" Hoglah exclaimed. Tirzah had the grace to feel ashamed as she blushed from her hairline to her nail beds. Noah, deciding to rescue her, gave her a hand, saying, "I guess having too many good cooks in this house has not given you a chance to show your skills. Let's get on with it before our guest becomes too famished." Mahlah wished she could ask Eitan some questions in private, but the cooking area was only about five feet from the sitting area. She and her uncle had observed this friction between Eitan and Tirzah several times and had commented on it. She did not tell their uncle about the encounter the two had had at the war in Arad, because it would expose Tirzah. She, however, perceived there was something else. Even though she had never been in love with a man, Mahlah feared that this was the case between Eitan and Tirzah. It was not a common thing these days for cousins to marry, she guessed because of the growth and expansion of the tribes, but it was not forbidden. Isaac and Rebekah were cousins, Jacob and his wives were cousins, to mention a few. And Eitan was indeed very eligible and attractive to any young woman. He was tall, handsome, and God-fearing. She had always loved him, as well as his brothers, but after what he had done for Tirzah at the battle front, he was more endeared to her. Noah and Tirzah did an excellent job fixing them lamb stew, baked manna, and a salad of cucumbers and melons. All through the evening, she watched Eitan try to engage Tirzah in a conversation directly, but she never responded with more than nods and shakes of her head. And she knew her sister very well, that her tongue was the pen of a very ready writer. She must be either so much in love that it made her shy or she was holding a grudge against Eitan. She was going to find out. The thought of Eitan and Tirzah as man and wife was not a bad idea. He was very capable of taking care of her both as wife and as a cousin. All her sisters seemed to be doing better in this department than she. She had never had any connection with any male other than her cousins. Even timid Noah had had men express interest in her several times. Was she too much of an old maid or did she put men off? Maybe they saw her as her sisters' keeper, which she was, and therefore regarded her as they would their mother. Because she was very protective of her sisters she was always scrutinizing every man that came close, and perhaps appeared standoffish. "I think it's time you worked on yourself, Mahlah!" She told herself.

## 29

THE CENSUS WAS OVER but the excitement was not. At the assembly, Moses was making known the results of the head count of men from every tribe that were to serve in the army. Despite all that they had been through with all the years of loss of lives, the results of the census was very impressive. Their total number was nearly the same as that of the first census that took place in the Desert of Sinai shortly after they had left Egypt. The Levites were not even included in this total number announced by Eleazar. Mahlah thought it was a miracle of numbers that had nothing to do with them but everything to do with the blessing of Abraham their father. More than this numerical strength, the issue of sharing the inheritance was paramount to a lot of them. Moses had told them that the larger tribes would receive larger shares and the decision of allocation of places would be by lot. Mahlah was convinced more than ever that this was the time to approach Moses. The elders had not gotten back to them as they had said, and Mahlah feared that they might never do so until everything was divided. During the census, her father's house had not even been noted, and by hierarchy, her father's house would have been numbered first among the Hepherite clan if he had sons. Mahlah rallied her sisters among the crowd and told them her decision. "Right now?" exclaimed Noah. "Yes now, put yourselves together while I quickly whisper to Uncle Baruch." After finding her uncle and letting him know their intention, Mahlah returned to her sisters. Arm in arm they moved forward to the front of the tent of meeting. As they made their way to the front, people turned to look at them suspiciously, like they were about to commit an abominable act. Tammuz moved quickly and close to Mahlah, her best friend, and whispered, "What are you doing?" "Move away, Tammuz, before you get involved," Mahlah replied, and watched her best friend stand still with a look of utter disbelief. They made it to the front and stood before Moses, Eleazar the new high priest, the tribal leaders, and the whole assembly. With their heads bowed in a show of respect, but their hearts beating erratically, they stood until Moses asked them to speak. "Thank you, great man of God. We are the daughters of Zelophehad, the son of Hepher of the Mannasseh tribe. Our father died in the desert. He was not among the followers of Korah who rebelled against the Lord. Our father died of his own sin and left no sons. Why should our father's name disappear from his clan because he had no son? Give us property among our father's relatives." As Mahlah said this, she could hear the people gasp and whisper behind her. She refused to give in to the fear that was rising from the pit of her gut. She kept her face straight, avoiding the leaders on the sides, and focused directly on Moses. She was not sure but thought she saw something that looked like a smile on his face and that gave her hope. Moses said to them, and indirectly to all the people who were watching and probably expecting some immediate punishment for their act, "This case is beyond me. I am going to take it before the Lord and will get back to you. Go in peace." Mahlah could not believe their fortune. They had made it. They had stood before Moses and the whole assembly and their petition had been heard. They had not been stoned. Moses did not even talk about their father's sin like the committee of elders had taken pleasure in reminding them. She had seen the look of shock on the faces of most of the leaders. Mahlah and her sisters left in disbelief and also in exhilaration. They walked majestically back to their tent, refusing to let the stares and side talks bother them. They had anticipated all these so they were not bothered. Mahlah knew that until Moses gave them a verdict, they would have to live down all the talk and sneers. They would have to keep away from public view, and she hoped that it would not take too long. Mahlah was so positive that they had won this case by the mere fact that they had made their petition and Moses was giving them special consideration. Contrary to the popular belief of her people, Mahlah believed that dealing with YHWH was better than dealing with men. Somewhere along her journey of faith, she'd come to know that he was like a father, something that no Israelite would dare contemplate. They believed they were all servants and YHWH was only to be obeyed and feared. Mahlah wondered what they would say of the way she often talked and even argued with YHWH, just like she would with her father.

The moment they got into their tent, they let out cries and shouts of joy. They hugged one another in tears. "I cannot believe we did it. Mahlah you spoke so boldly." Milcah grabbed her sister and kissed her. "Yes, we made it. Did you see the looks on the faces of the elders? Great Uncle Helek nearly collapsed at the point you said we wanted father's property." Tirzah was bubbling with excitement, tinged with a little spite. Great Uncle Helek was the only surviving one from the Gileadite clan and the oldest person in their tribe. "Let's give praise to the Lord for seeing us through. I know that he will give us a favorable verdict. Like a father, he pities us. He will not put us to shame because we have trusted in him," Mahlah led her sisters in thanksgiving.

## 30

They were at the tent of meeting again three days after their petition. This meeting had been called on their account. "I have taken your case to YHWH." There was a long pause, and Mahlah feared the worst, until Moses continued again, "He said your petition should be granted." There was a loud cheering from the women and there were expressions of disbelief from the men. Mahlah realized that they were not alone but other women in the camp may be facing the same dilemma. Yet when they had made their petition, these women had not shown any form of support, in fact they were the ones who had peddled the talk of their daring act. In the three days that followed their petition they heard all sorts of views expressed among their people. Most had condemned their act as insolent. Some had said it was a rebellion that should be punished like the others, likening it to Korah's rebellion. Serious hostility had emanated from their tribal men, who felt most threatened by their petition. Mahlah and her sisters were happy as they listened to the verdict, which was definitely worth all the hostility of the three days. "The Lord said that if a man dies and leaves no son, turn his inheritance to his daughter. If he has no daughter, give his inheritance over to his brothers. If he has no brothers, give his inheritance to his father's brothers. If his father has no brothers, give his inheritance to the nearest relative in his clan. This is to be a legal requirement for all Israelites." Moses finished giving the new law and proceeded to do something else that had them all overwhelmed with questions. Moses called for Joshua the son of Nun to come forward and announced that YHWH had appointed him to take his place. Joshua was going to lead them now to the promised land. They all watched in stunned silence as the ordination was performed, with Moses and Eleazar laying hands on Joshua.

"Is it really possible for anyone to take the place of Moses, or were we all just played?" Tirzah, who could never restrain her thoughts, asked as they walked back to their tent. This turn of events had overshadowed their matter, something Mahlah was glad about. "Daughters of courage, you have changed our destiny today. God bless you and may you go down in the history of this nation," an old woman they did not know came before them and pronounced in a whisper, looking warily about her as if she was being watched. Just as quickly as she had appeared the old woman left the girls wondering what her story was. They walked in silence the rest of the way to their tent. Tirzah, determined to talk about the matter that was now on every Israelite mind, continued, "Is Moses going to die? What do you think will become of us all?" After hundreds of years of oppression and suffering in the land of Egypt, it was Moses who had been appointed to deliver them from the hands of Pharaoh. It was Moses who owned a special staff that had given them miracle after miracle. When YHWH wanted to communicate anything to them, it was Moses he told. When they offended YHWH and would have been annihilated, it was Moses who pleaded on their behalf and saved them. Moses, as far as they were concerned, was second only to YHWH. Even more recently, had it not been for Moses, who in humility had taken their unusual case to YHWH, the sisters were sure they would have been denied. "YHWH knows what he is doing. He has always been the one in control. He chose Moses, and as unimaginable as it is to think of this journey without him, I believe YHWH will take care of everything," Mahlah answered her sister confidently, but inside she felt like their shelter was being taken away and they were being exposed. As grateful as she was that the ruling was in their favor, she would not mind exchanging this favor for Moses to remain, were it remotely possible. Since they got to Shittim on the other side of Jericho every one's hope has been high. They could smell, see, and even taste the promised land, but now with this new development, would the people be courageous enough to go ahead? Joshua was one the twelve spies sent to explore Canaan about forty years ago. He and Caleb had returned with encouraging news and strong belief that they could take the land while the other ten had discouraged the people. Joshua was a great captain who had led their army to several wins. When he was not on the battle field or on a mission, he was always with Moses. So she guessed he was the most qualified person to take over from Moses even though he was no kin. Hur, Miriam's son, who had practically acted like the next Moses since he had been ordained, would be disappointed. As for Moses' sons, they were never in the picture, being half Hebrew and half Midianite. "So Joshua has got to be the best," Mahlah reasoned.

"Are you in support of this idea, Uncle Baruch?" Mahlah asked in disbelief. It was a day after their victory and her uncle was visiting with not too palatable news. Their uncles and male cousins had held a meeting concerning the implications of their share in the inheritance, with the conclusion that Mahlah and her sisters must marry only within their tribe. They were planning to take their petition to Moses immediately. Mahlah was confused and angry but knew deep down, emotions aside, they were right. If she and her sisters married men from the other tribes, the land they inherited would automatically belong to the tribe they marry. It was no hidden secret that every tribe desired to possess the largest portion of the lands, but this was going to be determined by their numbers. The largest tribe according to the last census went with the largest portion. There was power in size. Their tribe was the sixth-largest tribe, with five other tribes ahead of them, Mahlah was sure they could not afford to go further down the ladder. "I wouldn't jump to conclusions if I were you, at least until the case is presented to Moses. You know that I will always look out for your interests, and I do not believe you and your sisters should be forced to marry your cousins and uncles, especially if you have other preferences." "Uncle, we do not have any prospective husbands in view, I am just concerned that this may be arising from greed and hostility. What if they are doing this just to punish us?" "Then they will not prevail. I came to let you know so you are not taken by surprise." "Thank you, father," Mahlah relented. "Then I leave you to warn your sisters and hope for the best."

Mahlah had expected Tirzah to be very vocal about this new development. Tirzah had been her greatest worry. Noah had always said she was alright with an arranged marriage. Milcah and Hoglah were very traditional and would be accepting of any situation imposed by their culture. So when Tirzah did not flare up, it became clearer to Mahlah that she was indeed in love with Eitan, and that the feeling was mutual. Mahlah ran through her mind the men she knew from their tribe. She would be more comfortable with a distant cousin than with any of Uncle Baruch's sons who were like brothers to her. "Tell me, Tirzah, would you accept Eitan as your husband?" Tirzah blushed and smiled but refused to answer her sister. "That settles you then," Mahlah said, and turned to her other sisters. "Milcah, Noah, and Hoglah, do you fancy any of the male relatives we know other than the Helekite clan?" The Helekite clan was a no-no for them. It was a cousin from this clan that had given their father away, leading to his premature death. "I do not think so right now. We need to do some searching," Hoglah answered good-naturedly.

They were back at the tent of meeting again, this time to hear the outcome of the petition made by the family heads of the tribe of Manasseh. Moses looked the same if not even more regal as he gave them another law, a follow-up to the one he had given yesterday. "What the tribes of the descendants of Joseph are saying is right. The Lord has commanded that the daughters of Zelophehad may marry anyone they please as long as they marry within the tribal clan of their father. No inheritance in Israel is to pass from tribe to tribe, for every Israelite shall keep the tribal land inherited from his forefathers." It was a win-win situation for them after all. Marrying their cousins meant that their father's name would remain forever. She felt more victorious than she had after the first verdict. Their uncles and cousins, for whatever reason, had become instruments to ensure that they would not lose their father's name in the process of marriage. It could not be any better than this. Mahlah's only challenge now was who among these relatives of hers would be a near match to her *Bashert*. Tirzah was fortunately in love with Eitan, the rest of them would have to hope for something close.

# 31

A SERIES OF OTHER ordinances were given them over the next few days. Everyone was anticipating the day Moses would no longer stand before them, but none could imagine him dying. From every indication it appeared that their great leader was putting his house in order as he gave them more and more instructions. Among those instructions came one that was devastating for his wife, Zipporah. The Israelite army was to take vengeance on the Midianites for their involvement with King Balak, who had tried to curse them, and for also seducing their men. Moses was sending twelve thousand soldiers, a thousand from each tribe, to attack the Midianites. Phinehas, the son of Eleazar, the high priest, would go with them, carrying articles from the sanctuary representing divine Presence. As a result, the camp was full of activity. Each tribe was busy with selecting and preparing the best of their men to represent them. Eitan was one of those men from the tribe of Manasseh. Tirzah was afraid for Eitan and she did not hide this fact from her sisters. Since Mahlah confronted her with the question of her feelings for Eitan, she had realized the truth herself and stopped fighting what was meant to be. Eitan for a long time had been confronting her with the fact that they were in love and should do something about it, but Tirzah had fought it for a long time until fate has made it inevitable. She'd argued with herself that Eitan was too close for comfort, hoping to fall in love with another man from the tribe of Judah. The men of Judah were the bravest of the Israelites. After the pronouncement by Moses that they were to marry from their tribe alone, Eitan had proposed to her immediately, saying he was no longer going to pretend about his feelings. She had for the first time yielded to his advances and was so happy now except for this war with the Midianites. She knew how capable Eitan was in battle, having witnessed it firsthand, but nevertheless she worried that anything could happen. As for the outcome of the war, YHWH had guaranteed them victory because he was the one sending them, but her fear was of casualty. Eitan's brother, Adiel, was a victim of war and to date could not use one of his limbs again. She wanted Eitan to return to her intact, just as he was. Now that they had found each other, she could not imagine life without him, and it did not matter that they had just discovered that love. "Can you believe that father's cousin Alon made advances at me? The man is older than father would have been had he been alive," Hoglah was complaining to her sisters. "Maybe he was wooing you for his son," Noah said, always the last to believe a bad report of anybody. "But then you know that he has a right," Mahlah stated as a matter of fact. "That is why we ought to thank the Lord for giving us a choice. Moses said we were free to marry anyone we please, so if you do not consent to him, that's the end," Mahlah reminded her sister. "I have been waiting to tell you all this. I want to go with Adiel, if he will have me," Noah announced, shocking her sisters. "Why, for pity or for love?" Tirzah questioned. "I am convinced that it will please YHWH and Uncle Baruch, you all know that his betrothal was broken because of his injury and no maiden in this camp will have him," Noah replied. "So then it is out of sympathy you want to do this. I wish I could do something like that but I want love and passion," Hoglah rolled her eyes as she said this. "Milcah, you have been awfully quiet about all of this. Do you have anyone in mind?" Mahlah asked, wanting to carry everyone along, wishing they could all tie the knot at the same time. "I just miss father and mother. I do not like this arrangement. I wish father were still here, I know he would agree with me." They were all surprised by Milcah's outburst, and Mahlah feared she may have given her heart to another man from another tribe. "Are you in love with someone? You know father and mother would be very happy and proud of us right now. This has always been father's dream. That was why he wanted male children so badly." Mahlah held her sister's hands and looked into her face as she said this. Milcah started sobbing badly. "I know, but it is just that I am unhappy, I have been since Ami broke my heart, and I just cannot see any man in

Manasseh that can take his place." "But the Benjamite was unfaithful and he is dead now!" a perplexed Tirzah exclaimed. "Sshhhh, you do not have to remind her. I understand Milcah," Noah said to make Milcah feel better. Mahlah felt sorry for Milcah and she felt guilty that she had not noticed the state of her sister's emotion. She had been too taken with the excitement of winning and it was too late to do anything now. The command had been given, they could not disobey. She had thought that Milcah, like Noah, would go along with anything imposed by culture, but Milcah definitely wanted more. She would have to spend time to encourage her to find someone in their tribe that she could fall in love with. This was the price they had to pay for their inheritance, nothing good comes cheap, they say. She was going to see Tammuz right away. She had decided that she would employ her best friend's services in this matter. Tammuz seemed to know more of who was who in their tribe even though she belonged to the tribe of Ephraim. The last time they were together, Tammuz her friend had helped enumerated a list of her male relatives she believed were eligible and right for Mahlah. The thought of it all brought a smile to Mahlah's face. Some months back they had not known what direction to take as concerning marriage. Now they were being regarded as jewels of great value, desirable by every man in the tribe of Manasseh. She believed that since YHWH commanded this, He also had prepared their husbands for them. All they needed now was guidance to discover them. Tirzah and Noah's had already been revealed, so definitely he would reveal those for Hoglah, Milcah, and herself.

The war went well in their favor. The twelve thousand soldiers that went all returned with very few casualties and with a lot of captives and plunder. They had killed the five kings of Midian, as well as Balaam the prophet that the King of Moab had hired to place a curse on Israel. Moses and Eleazar would not allow the soldiers come into the camp, but the whole assembly went to welcome them outside the camp by the River of Jordan. The spoils of war that they brought with them were unbelievable. There were Midianite women and children everywhere. They had large herds and flocks of animals carrying on their backs items of silver and gold. Moses was not pleased with the captives they brought back. "Why have you allowed the women to live? They were the ones who followed Balaam's advice and were the means of turning Israelites away from YHWH. Remember what happened at Peor when a plague struck down twenty-four thousand of your people because of them." The people immediately knew that they could not afford for that to happen again. The only option was to get rid of them. All the women and boys were put to the sword, but the young girls were saved, as instructed. It was a horrible sight, but a necessary evil to prevent a repetition of what had happened at Peor.

After all the excitement of the victory won, Moses announced again to them that he would not be going to the promised land with them but was going to be gathered unto his people. He gave the Transjordan land to the Reubenites and Gadites, who had lobbied for them, but made them vow to help the other tribes take over the remaining land before they settled on their land. There was a great weight of grief in the hearts of all the people for their leader. Moses was all they had ever known. He was the one they trusted to hear from YHWH without any questions. He has been a true father and shepherd of Israel. He was so humble and had truly cared for them, even sacrificing his family for them. The soldiers had actually wanted to do Moses' wife a favor by preserving some of her people, especially the women who could have been her sisters or their daughters. And when the Lord spoke otherwise they had been impressed by their leader's ability to put them, the people, first. Even his death was more of a sacrifice for them, because it was as a result of their disobedience. Moses told them that since the time he had ordained Joshua, he had pleaded with the Lord to allow him go with them to the promised land, but the Lord would not listen but instead would allow him only a look. Moses continued to give orders about everything to Eleazar and Joshua, and to the family heads of the Israelite tribes. He prayed for them and blessed them greatly and then prepared to go to the top of Mount Pigsah where he would see all of the promised land that he will not partake of. Moses had said that he was at peace with everything and was glad to be going to the real promised land whose sole architect was YHWH. Mahlah was overwhelmed with emotions at the point he said this. She was comforted as she wept and laughed at the same time.

The house of Zelophehad was at peace because YHWH had justified them. Tirzah and Noah were getting ready for their *Kiddushin*-betrothals to their cousins from the house of their dearest uncle Baruch.

They were all very happy, everything having turned out well for them. They were their father's heirs now, and she could imagine her father looking down, at peace now because his house was not left desolate after all.

## About the Book

Five girls born to a fourth-generation firstborn male during the exodus, in the time of Moses, struggle to survive in a world dominated by men. They refuse to be suffocated by traditions and spew out courage, changing their world and making history.

We see the journey to the promised land and the survival of the Israelites from a different perspective through the eyes of Zelophehad, a disappointed father, and his five courageous daughters.

This is a great read that brings life and color to an obscure story in the Bible. What did it mean to journey in the wilderness as a family for forty years with Moses during the exodus? Find out in *Their Father's Heirs*.

## About the Author

Cynthia Ekoh is a medical doctor from Africa who resides in the United States with her husband, a pastor. Her mission is to elaborate obscure stories in the Bible in such a colorful manner that you can relive the stories.

www.ingramcontent.com/pod-product-compliance
Lightning Source LLC
Chambersburg PA
CBHW070920160426
43193CB00011B/1543